RAISED BED REVOLUTION

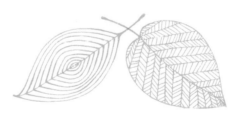

Brimming with creative inspiration, how-to projects, and useful information to enrich your everyday life, Quarto Knows is a favorite destination for those pursuing their interests and passions. Visit our site and dig deeper with our books into your area of interest: Quarto Creates, Quarto Cooks, Quarto Homes, Quarto Lives, Quarto Drives, Quarto Explores, Quarto Gifts, or Quarto Kids.

First published in 2016 by Cool Springs Press, an imprint of The Quarto Group, 100 Cummings Center, Suite 265-D, Beverly, MA 01915, USA. T (978) 282-9590 F (978) 283-2742 QuartoKnows.com

Cool Springs Press titles are also available at discount for retail, wholesale, promotional, and bulk purchase. For details, contact the Special Sales Manager by email at specialsales@quarto.com or by mail at The Quarto Group, Attn: Special Sales Manager, 100 Cummings Center, Suite 265-D, Beverly, MA 01915, USA.

10

ISBN: 978-1-59186-650-3

Library of Congress Cataloging-in-Publication Data

Nolan, Tara, 1977- author.
Raised bed revolution : build it, fill it, plant it ... garden
  anywhere / Tara Nolan.
Minneapolis, MN : Cool Springs Press, 2016.
LCCN 2015047450 | ISBN 9781591866503 (hc)
LCSH: Beds (Gardens) | Raised bed gardening.
LCC SB423.7 .N65 2016 | DDC 635.9/62--dc23
LC record available at http://lccn.loc.gov/2015047450

Acquiring Editor: **Mark Johanson**
Project Manager: **Alyssa Bluhm**
Art Director: **Cindy Samargia Laun**
Book Design and Layout: **Amelia LeBarron**
Lead Photographer: **Donna Griffith**
Builder: **Scott McKinnon**
Illustration: **Len Churchill**
Cover photo courtesy of **Bonnie Plants**. Photo by **Van Chaplin**.

Printed in China

PHOTO CREDITS
Greg Maxson: 257
Crystal Liepa: 54 (top)
Paul Markert: 53
Rau + Barber: 126, 188-193, 258, 261
Shutterstock: 25, 42, 43 (both), 44, 45 (both), 46 (both), 47 (both),
    48 (top right), 63 (bottom), 66, 68 (both), 70, 94, 117 (bottom), 124 (top),
    134 (left), 137 (left, both), 151 (top left), 167 (all), 175, 178, 181 (top, both),
    237 (top left), 148 (top), 254 (bottom left), 255 (bottom left), 256 (top left)
Van Chaplin/Bonnie Plants: cover

RAISED BED REVOLUTION

BUILD IT, FILL IT, PLANT IT . . .
Garden Anywhere!

TARA NOLAN

COOL
SPRINGS
PRESS

TO MY LOVING, SUPPORTIVE FAMILY
AND GENEROUS NETWORK OF GARDENER FRIENDS.

ACKNOWLEDGMENTS

Raised Bed Revolution has been the most fun, fulfilling project I've ever worked on, but it's also been the most challenging of my career. None of what you see throughout these pages would have been possible without the help of several generous people—some whom I've met in person and others whom I've only met via close-knit gardening pockets of the Internet and social media (how cool is that?). Here's my list of fabulous people who deserve great big thank-yous:

To my editor, Mark Johanson, for entrusting me with this gift, for your patience in dealing with a newbie book author, and for making this huge project come together. To my art director, Cindy Laun, for taking my words, photos, and sidebar ideas and magically transforming them into this beautiful book.

Writing and creating the projects for *Raised Bed Revolution* was quite literally a family affair. To my husband, Rich Auger, for supporting all my crafty, creative dreams, for building me my first raised beds, and for all your help in the garden and around the house with whatever needed to be done during the whole process. A massive thank-you to my parents, Bill and Wendy, and to my sister and brother-in-law, Hilary and Deon, who helped me in my own garden and provided yard space for some of the beds, and planted and tended them so they looked lush and camera-ready. Deon also helped me figure out how to build a cold frame. And a special thank-you to my niece Isla (who was three years old throughout the project) for providing updates and taste-testing what was planted in her parents' raised beds, especially cilantro and "the one that tastes like licorice."

To Niki Jabbour, for all your photos and ideas, and for coaching me through this whole book-writing process. You are truly a selfless, generous, amazing mentor. And to my other two Savvy Gardening sidekicks, Amy Andrychowicz and Jessica Walliser, for your photos, ideas, and support. I'm so incredibly lucky to have all three of you in my life!

To my builder, Scott McKinnon, whom I met serendipitously through mountain biking, another passion of mine. Scott is the super-talented carpenter who designed and built many of the projects you see in this book.

To Donna Griffith (and the fabulous assistants who accompanied you to all the photo shoots—Leila Ashtari, Stuart Blaine, and Lisa Daly). I've admired your work in magazines for years, and I'm so honored that your gorgeous photography and style is featured throughout my book.

To Len Churchill, whom I met when I wore my editor's hat at *Canadian Home Workshop* magazine, for your beautiful technical illustrations.

To Jenny Rhodenizer and Paul Zammit at the Toronto Botanical Garden, for all your continued support and for allowing me to showcase one of my raised beds in your gorgeous gardens.

To all those in my garden-writing realm who sat down for coffee, facilitated introductions, or shared your photos and projects: Tracey Ayton, Karen Bertelsen, Steven Biggs, Beth Billstrom, Jamie Bussin, Jennifer Connell, Kristin Crouch, Hilary Dahl and Colin McCrate, Johanne Daoust, Donna Dawson, Marie Eisenmann, Lorraine Flanigan, Brenda Franklin, Trish Fry, Shawn Gallaugher, Jamie Gilgen, Marc Green and Arlene Hazzan Green, Bren Haas, Michael Holmes, Andrea Hungerford, Sean James, Verna Kakowchyk, Signe Langford, Meighan Makarchuk, Narmin Moloo, Dee Nash, Brandon Park, Susan Poizner, Alex Rochon-Terry, Candy Venni, Rick Weingarden, Melissa J. Will, and Ian Wilson. Also thanks to Fairmont Hotels & Resorts, Proven Winners, the University of Maryland Extension, and Woolly Pocket.

To the amazing companies that provided me with materials, plants, and plans for the book: Bonnie Plants, Conquest Steel, Freedom Growing, Gardener's Supply Company, and Loblaw Companies.

And to my MacBook, for not dying on me and losing my work, even though it seemed like you wanted to quit. Often. I may now allow you to retire in dignity.

CONTENTS

WHAT IS THE RAISED BED REVOLUTION?

When you hear the word *revolution*, what comes to mind? You probably think of the more common definition, which is "rebellion" or "uprising," right? But *revolution* also means "innovation" and "modernization." For the purpose of this discussion—and for this whole book, for that matter—let's focus on those last two words.

The emphasis on eating fresh, local food over the past few years has really changed the landscape of our towns and cities. Not only are farmers' markets more popular than ever before, more and more people are deciding to put their green thumbs to the test and grow their own food at home.

This is where innovation and modernization come into play.

Raised beds aren't a new invention, but they have certainly become more prevalent with this movement to grow fresh produce. And they've helped to modernize the way we garden. In bigger yards, raised beds seem to have replaced the typical expanse of a veggie plot. What's more, gardeners have gotten creative over the years and are experimenting with different options. This burst of innovation means a raised bed may not be a typical rectangle shape built from timber.

In fact, raised beds can be made in all shapes and styles—rectangles, squares, triangles, and circles; ankle- and waist-height; wooden and stone construction. They can even be welded out of steel, aging to a nice rust-colored patina over time, or made out of corrugated sheets of steel inset in a wood frame. Creative DIYers are rescuing materials from scrap heaps, antique markets, behind sheds, and underneath decks to upcycle into raised beds. Commonly found items, such as washbasins, stock tanks, and recycling bins, are getting a new lease on life as ready-made gardens.

As the types of beds have changed, so have their locations. Raised beds are no longer just confined to the backyard. They're appearing on front and side lawns of residential streets,

spaces that were once reserved solely for grass or ornamental plantings. Homeowners are reaping the benefits of that extra space and growing food to feed their families. Often the front yard becomes the prime candidate for a raised bed because that's the spot on the property with the best growing conditions—lots of hot sun! But savvy gardeners are taking advantage of whatever locations they can find.

Raised beds also are appearing in school and community gardens as well as in botanical and public gardens—often with accompanying seminars to teach people how to build and plant them. And if you peek behind a restaurant or look at a local eatery's rooftop, there's a good chance you'll catch a glimpse of a variety of raised beds where chefs have easy access to fresh herbs and a host of other menu-worthy edibles.

You may have started to see a newer type of raised bed here and there. Called "enabling gardens," they provide accessible growing spaces and inspiration to those who have various limitations. They help people with cognitive or physical disabilities enjoy the peace, motivation, and satisfaction that come from gardening.

LEFT: My first raised beds, ready to be installed in their new home. *Tara Nolan*

ABOVE: The first two raised beds filled with soil and ready to plant with garlic. *Tara Nolan*

Raised beds have also become instructional tools. Inner-city organizations are pairing them with educational programming to teach children who live in dense, urban areas where food comes from. Urban grocers and farmers' markets show enthusiastic new green thumbs how to garden for the first time, inspiring them to test their skills with edibles. Then, at the end of the season, they teach excited gardeners what they can do with their fresh bounty by offering a range of classes, from canning and preserving to incorporating fresh produce into healthy recipes.

Food banks also have benefitted from the increased use of raised beds for growing edibles. Individuals as well as organizations and community gardens often donate their extra bounty to feed the less fortunate.

The increased excitement for growing edibles has resulted in more interesting varieties of plants available at local nurseries, garden centers, and

grocery stores. Edibles that once had to be grown from seed are being introduced to the masses in the form of plants. And an increasing selection of patio plants allows those with minuscule spaces to grow everything from tomatoes to mini melons.

Which leads to one very important detail about owning raised beds: they prove you don't necessarily need a conventional yard to grow a row of tomatoes. Because you're filling raised beds with your own mix of fresh, nutrient-rich soil, they can sit on gravel, pavement, poor soil, rooftops—pretty much anywhere!

Yards that were deemed to be hostile growing environments, with hard-packed clay or even sand, as well as patio stones, driveways, and decks, are no longer off-limits. You can place a raised bed right on them and fill it with quality soil.

LEFT: Some of the most interesting raised beds you'll see are actually built from kits. *Donna Griffith*

BELOW: Raised beds can be added to any backyard in a configuration that suits the available space. Built-in trellis systems provide no-fuss support to vining plants. *Hilary Dahl for Seattle Urban Farm Co.*

And let's not forget that a great deal of the population lives in urban spaces—or subdivisions with postage-stamp-sized lots. Rooftops, balconies, and teeny, tiny patios have all become fair game when it comes to locations for growing your own food. This means that gardeners may have to get creative when it comes to what they're planting in, but options abound. There are all sorts of compact raised beds that can be placed out of the way in a sunny corner. Some even have self-watering systems in place, so they require even less maintenance.

RIGHT: Planting ornamental blooms near your raised beds not only adds visual interest to the area, they attract valuable pollinators too. *Bren Haas*

BELOW: Raised beds have introduced the concept of small-scale farming to urban backyards. *Marc Green, Arlene Hazzan Green, The Backyard Urban Farm Company*

Vertical gardening has become a popular concept that enables eager green thumbs to grow up where there is limited space. Different wall contraptions that provide space to grow fresh greens, edible blooms, and herbs are basically micro-sized versions of raised beds set up vertically rather than horizontally to take advantage of a sunny locale.

The aim of this book is not to reinvent the wheel but rather to inspire you with tons of ideas, practical tips, and easy-to-follow project plans that will help you create your own raised beds—

LEFT: The beauty of raised beds is that they don't have to be placed directly on soil. You can set them on a driveway or a patch of gravel, and then fill them with healthy soil. *Steven Biggs*

BELOW: If you're not handy with tools and construction, you can use found items, like tree trunks or discarded rocks, to shore up the sides of a raised bed. *Niki Jabbour*

no matter the size of your space. And if you don't happen to be particularly handy, there's an entire chapter devoted just to you. There are endless options for upcycling materials, from abandoned basins to whiskey barrels. Really, the only limit is your imagination.

This book will also introduce you to experts who share their tips on topics ranging from soil to irrigation, growing throughout the winter, and attracting pollinators to the garden. Be prepared to be inspired by hundreds of images that are meant to show you what a wonderful addition raised beds can be to your garden.

So, whether you have a big yard or a tiny balcony, join the raised bed revolution and create a bed—or two or three!—that allows you to reap the benefits of a fresh, homegrown harvest.

You don't even need to live on solid ground to have a raised bed. A balcony, terrace, or rooftop will do, provided you have the necessary growing conditions. *Marc Green, Arlene Hazzan Green, The Backyard Urban Farm Company*

HOW I JOINED
THE RAISED BED REVOLUTION

My first raised beds were happy surprises. After spending our first growing season getting used to a new home and a new property, my husband and I decided that we wanted to tidy up the area of the yard that played host to a traditional, in-ground vegetable garden. We had been researching raised beds online to figure out how to build them. Then I happened to go away one weekend, and when I came back, there were two brand-new cedar raised beds in the backyard.

We promptly got them settled in the old garden and arranged for a soil delivery. I planted my first crop just a couple of weeks later. It was autumn, so the perfect time of year to plant a whole bunch of garlic (an item that is often on my grocery list). And then, as soon as I could get outside to garden in the spring, I filled the rest of the space in the beds with an assortment of veggies, including sweet peas, peppers, tomatoes, and onions, and some ornamental zinnias as well.

In creating this book, my raised bed collection has grown immensely. I now have four big raised beds, a cold frame, a lettuce table, and about five other smaller-scale raised beds made from upcycling found items and materials—not to mention all the pots I put together each year. This means more fresh fruit, vegetables, and herbs that I can harvest throughout the year to eat right away or preserve. There's nothing better than dashing out the back door to snip a handful of lettuce and herbs for a salad, or picking a ripe heirloom tomato to add to a summer burger. I also love drying herbs from my raised beds for tea and my spice rack, whipping up different pestos to freeze into cubes for hearty winter pasta meals, and making jams and jellies so that I can enjoy summer produce in the dead of winter. All of this fresh produce is grown in raised beds.

Through all my research, I've discovered countless others who have also discovered the immense satisfaction of growing edibles (and ornamentals) in raised beds. Raised beds really do allow you to garden anywhere, whether it be in a backyard or community plot, or on a deserted piece of land or a wee patio, or up in the sky on a balcony or rooftop.

— Tara Nolan

Share photos of your raised beds on Facebook (www.facebook.com/raisedbedrevolution) or on Twitter and Instagram, using this hashtag: #raisedbedrevolution.

I grow a lot of edible plants from seed, but I'll also grab plants from local nurseries to fill in the spaces!
Donna Griffith

THE RISE IN EDIBLE GARDENING INTEREST

There has definitely been a shift in how we garden over the last several years. While some creative and persistent green thumbs have always overcome the challenge of planting in any space, veggie gardens were predominantly relegated to a back corner of the garden in our collective mindsets until fairly recently. But as the awareness of where our food comes from went from being a hippie notion to a popular culture concern, we began to see articles about edibles everywhere. The terms *fresh, local,* and *organic* quickly became pervasive buzzwords used in restaurants, from fancy dining experiences to small, casual cafes, as well as in grocery stores. Farmers' markets started popping up (or existing ones became more popular) with visitors being encouraged to meet the farmers who grew their produce. Supermarket customers were suddenly requesting fruits and vegetables that were grown within a certain radius of where they live. Community-shared agriculture (CSA) and organic delivery services were growing a healthy subscription base.

All of this attention on fresh, local produce has resulted in new gardeners tentatively testing out their green thumbs by growing their own food for the first time. And it has been a boon to more experienced gardeners, because garden centers and nurseries have caught on and now offer a greater variety of interesting edibles that might not have been available before. Those who are really ambitious seek out interesting heirloom seeds to grow and get started on the gardening season in January when the catalogs come out.

LEFT: A vegetable garden can get a little chaotic. Raised beds are a good solution to maintain some control. *Hilary Dahl for Seattle Urban Farm Co.*

Yet it's not like raised beds are a completely new invention. However, they have a way of making edible gardening seem more attainable. And easy. And fun. You can plunk a raised bed anywhere (as long as it's in the sun). And in a grouping, raised beds look neat and tidy, whether they're in a front, back, or side yard, or in the corner of a deck.

Handy or not, anyone can own a raised bed and grow fresh food to put on the table each day. There are so many options from kits and DIY projects to fabric pots the size of a small veggie plot. Kid-friendly tools and seed packets get young green thumbs digging in the dirt at a young age and also help them appreciate where their food comes from.

WHERE TO FIND YOUR RAISED BED INSPIRATION

Your own neighborhood is a great place to start. Check out local community gardens or neighbors who have staged their raised beds in the front yard. Recreation centers, churches, parks— all these public spaces may have raised beds too. If you're fortunate to live near a public garden, check it out. It used to be that the blooms took center stage at a botanical garden. However, with people more aware these days of where the food they consume comes from, creative staff and horticulturists are introducing edibles into a landscape that was once dominated by ornamentals. It's worth a stroll through these gardens to see if you can gather ideas on what to grow as well as designs for raised beds.

Of course, surfing the web can also unveil a treasure-trove of Pinterest-worthy ideas.

If you're not really into picking up a hammer— or you simply don't have the space or tools to build something—there are some amazing kits you can order that take the guesswork out of a raised bed project. You simply choose the design you want and wait for it to arrive in the mail, detailed instructions and all! Some don't require any assembly; a fabric garden, for example, simply needs to be unfolded and filled with fresh soil. Other raised bed kits might call for a screwdriver, power drill, or hammer to put them together. Ask a neighbor if you can borrow some tools if you don't own a toolbox.

With a little creative digging, you'll unearth a ton of ideas that suit your space, purpose, and skill level.

Community gardens can be a great source of fresh raised bed ideas. *Niki Jabbour*

SPROUTING RAISED BED COMPANIES

Entrepreneurial green thumbs, keen to share their love of growing, are forming companies that will build raised beds for clients, and they may even pass on a few tips in the process. After working on farms at home and abroad, Ian Wilson launched Portland Edible Gardens in 2013. He says he started the company because he'd had numerous people tell him they wanted to grow their own food, but they had no idea where to start. Not only does Ian and his team build beds, they customize planting plans for their customers.

Ian Wilson of Portland Edible Gardens is making his mark on his community one raised bed at a time. *Ian Wilson*

Freedom Growing, the company that supplied the kit for the colorful raised bed on page 144, started out making greenhouses but clearly saw an opportunity in the market to build a unique style of raised bed. Each kit comes with easy-to-follow instructions, all the materials necessary to build the bed (all you need are a couple of tools), and a packet of recipe cards that feature different planting combinations.

In other words, it's clear that companies not only care about selling their products, they want to inspire new and experienced gardeners to get the most out of their new raised beds and have success with their gardens.

OVERCOMING THE CHALLENGE OF A SMALL, URBAN SPACE

Rooftops, balconies, small patios, postage-stamp-sized lawns. These are not obstacles when it comes to raised bed gardening—unless those spaces receive absolutely no sunshine. In that case, you might want to look into signing up for a community garden plot to grow your own produce. But, if you get a reasonable amount of sunshine in a teeny, tiny space (six to eight hours a day), you can grow food. In fact, you'd be amazed at how much you can grow in a limited area.

Mini versions of raised beds can be built to fit a small space. Or, get creative and upcycle a wooden wine box or old apple crate. Recycling bins can produce a potato crop that you can store over the winter, and easy-to-make projects, such as a lettuce table, can keep you stocked up on freshly snipped salad for weeks! Furthermore, there are lots of kits and ready-to-plant options available that are tailored to urban living and small-space growing conditions.

The trick for small-space gardening is to look for patio varieties of plants that won't take over a space. Look for interesting edibles, such as mini-melons, cucumbers, and peppers. These plants are bred to be smaller, but there will be a greater concentration of fruit and veggies on a more compact plant. Also, train your harvest to reach towards the sky. Beans, peas, cucumbers, and any other vining, climbing edibles can be trained up a trellis, obelisk, or other creative plant support. It's a great way to maximize space and reap a sizable harvest. And there are all sorts of irrigation options these days that will prevent you from having to water twice a day in the heat of summer.

Even 5-gallon buckets, which are easy to find at home improvement stores, can be turned into raised beds for edibles. Place them on a sunny driveway or corner of a patio if space is an issue. Wrapping them in burlap adds a decorative touch. *Donna Griffith*

RAISED BEDS
FEEDING COMMUNITIES

Community garden plots have been around for a long time, but many new spaces are being carved out for them on abandoned municipal lots and church properties, in parks, and near community centers, and other public spaces. Raised beds are a great way to keep plots neat and tidy, especially if they're all assigned to separate gardeners. With this proliferation of raised beds dotting communities, harvests can be too big for one family to consume. Many gardeners are donating large portions of their harvests to local

This garden was created for the members of a Boys & Girls Club chapter to work in during their before- and after-school programs. The neighborhood is in a densely populated urban area. A derelict parking lot was magically transformed into an educational—and entertaining—garden. The kids were called upon to get their hands dirty and plant the gardens. Seeds and seedlings were added to the various raised beds, each one with a theme. For example, a Superhero Garden featured spinach, kale, and other veggies that would help the kids grow big and strong. The aim of the project was to show the kids where their food comes from, allow them to tend the gardens all season long, and enjoy the fresh produce that they grew. *Tara Nolan*

food banks. This fresh produce supplements the boxed and canned goods a food bank will distribute to clients.

There are also after-school programs being formed that are incorporating programming to inspire young gardeners.

If you want to donate some of your backyard harvest, contact your local food bank to see how it handles fresh-food donations.

This urban farm is located on the roof of a homeless shelter. The abundance of vegetables, herbs, and edible flowers grown in this 6,000-square-foot garden—about one-and-a-half tons per season—makes its way down to the shelter's kitchens where it's used to feed the people who are welcomed through its doors. The project was initiated by Les Urbainculteurs, the company that also supplied the fabric gardening pots (called Smart Pots) that hold the plants for this urban farm. *Tara Nolan*

"One of the biggest stresses vegetable gardeners face is wasting produce," says Karen Bertelsen, who blogs about her community garden at *The Art of Doing Stuff.* "Every year I try to do whatever possible to make sure this doesn't happen. I can, I freeze, I dry, I eat. Most gardeners also give a lot of food away to ensure nothing rots and goes in the garbage. In 2015, the members of our community garden decided to see how much we could donate to our local food bank by making sure anything extra went to them. By the end of our first summer doing this, the food bank had received almost 4,000 servings of food from our gardens."
Karen Bertelsen

THE HAMILTON VICTORY GARDENS

The Hamilton Victory Gardens, located in Hamilton, Ontario, is a nonprofit, volunteer-based organization that turns vacant patches of urban land into productive, sustainable edible gardens. According to founders Bill and Judy Wilcox, the name and the project were inspired by the victory gardens that were created during World War II to feed communities and support the war effort. In this day and age, these gardens are fighting the war on poverty and nutrition.

Hamilton Victory Gardens donates all of its produce to local food programs. In fact, between 2011 when the organization first launched and the end of 2014, almost 100,000 pounds of fresh produce had been donated to local food banks.

The organization relies on the kindness and enthusiasm of volunteers to plant and maintain these gardens. Most of the raised beds have been built using simple concrete block formations and are filled with triple mix soil. Local companies supply these essential materials, and seeds are donated by a local supplier.

Currently, there are about a dozen gardens, each with several raised beds, set up on a variety of sites ranging from churches and community centers to city- and company-owned properties. There's even a garden on the property of a seniors' residence, with extra-wide pathways that allow for walkers, wheelchairs, and scooters, so residents can enjoy the gardens too.

One inner-city area that hosts a garden has been designated as a food desert, meaning that its inhabitants, many of whom live in subsidized housing, have to travel at least 2 miles to get to the nearest grocery store. The closest place to shop is a convenience store with inflated prices. Besides donating a great deal of its produce, this particular location provides access to fresh produce for locals at low prices during a Saturday morning farmers' market.

The Hamilton Victory Gardens' motto is "Let everyone, big and small, young and old, come together to help provide for others." This is an inspiring model that can be replicated in any community.

LEFT: Dozens of volunteers donate their time to build and tend the Hamilton Victory Gardens' raised beds. Produce from the gardens will feed the less fortunate. *Tara Nolan*

OPPOSITE: Community organizations use raised beds to create productive community gardens on sites with poor or contaminated soil—or even parking lots with no soil at all.

CHAPTER 1

GALLERY OF RAISED BEDS

Here's a little inspiration to get you started on the path to having your own raised beds.

LEFT: A metal archway secured to two raised beds curves over a pathway and lifts vining vegetables up and away from the soil. This helps prevent them from rotting and getting eaten by pests. It also makes for a cool-looking garden because the vegetables become an ornamental feature. *Jessica Walliser*

RIGHT: Not only do cabbages fill in a raised bed and crowd out weeds, they also make for very attractive plants that could hold their own in a perennial garden. Think of all the ornamental cabbages you see in garden centers come autumn. If you plant edible ones, they not only make a lovely border, but they can also be eaten! *Karen Bertelsen*

ABOVE: A larger raised bed in the Governor's Garden at the Historic Gardens in Annapolis Royal, Nova Scotia, is a historically accurate representation of an eighteenth-century raised bed garden. It features a handy pathway that ensures the gardeners who plant and weed will not be stepping into the beds. *Trish Fry*

LEFT: Wide pathways and flat surfaces mean that wheelchairs and walkers can easily maneuver around the raised beds at the Historic Gardens in Annapolis Royal, Nova Scotia. *Trish Fry*

RIGHT: A colorful shed and multiple climbing plants make this raised bed area feel like a green-filled alcove pulled from the pages of *The Secret Garden*. *Lorraine Flanigan*

BELOW: Raised beds can be colorful, lively additions to a backyard. *Amy Andrychowicz*

ABOVE: If you're building a raised bed out of wood, other materials can be used to complement the frame. *Niki Jabbour*

RIGHT: This raised bed contains gardens within a garden. Multiple pots filled with a variety of blooms and vegetables are carefully arranged. The garden shed provides a whole other level of garden envy. *Lorraine Flanigan*

OPPOSITE: This kitchen garden at Beechwood Gardens in Johannesburg, South Africa, offers multiple points of inspiration, from the orderly raised beds made of stone to the obelisks and potscaping. *Donna Dawson*

ABOVE: A raised bed in the middle of a field? Why not? This thriving garden proves that you can set up a raised bed anywhere, as long as the right conditions are in place. © Les Urbainculteurs / Smart Pots

RIGHT: Raised beds not only sprawl outward, but they can also sprawl upward with some help, maximizing any bit of space that will be hospitable enough for a garden.
© Les Urbainculteurs / Smart Pots

This chicken coop gives new meaning to the idea of "rooftop gardening."
Tara Nolan

ABOVE: A clever arch trains squash plants to grow upward, granting more space to other edibles that otherwise would not have fit in the garden.
Amy Andrychowicz

LEFT: No assembly required: Natural barriers, including logs and big rocks, have been used to outline raised bed areas.
Niki Jabbour

LEFT: Even a barrel tucked into a seemingly unusable corner of the garden can yield a generous crop. *Donna Griffith*

TOP: Row cover or plastic sheeting allows gardeners to get a head start on their crops earlier in the springtime. *Meighan Makarchuk*

ABOVE: The Square Foot Gardening method works especially well when planting an assortment of leafy greens. *Meighan Makarchuk*

This extensive collection of raised beds built by Andrea Hungerford, who founded the blog *On Blueberry Hill*, uses the same type of corrugated steel that was used to create the raised bed on page 152. Wood is used to build the shape of the structure; steel pieces are used to make the ends and sides. You can see that Hungerford has also used stock tanks as raised beds in her garden! *Andrea Hungerford*

ABOVE: Garden communicator Bren Haas has used a stacked timber design to build a collection of raised beds in her yard. Haas, the host of the popular weekly @TheGardenChat (#gardenchat) on Twitter, has surrounded a sizable greenhouse with her raised beds and a series of pots, all containing a mix of annuals and perennials, both edible and ornamental. In the winter, some of these beds are transformed into cold frames with triangular covers that keep the contents warm enough to survive. *Bren Haas*

RIGHT: You may be wondering why there's a tarp suspended over some of the raised beds in this garden. The cover was intended to protect tomatoes from late blight and was eventually folded up to let the sun in. *Kristin Crouch*

LEFT: Add some visual interest to a collection of raised beds by including different shapes and sizes. Here, a half-barrel acts as a raised bed and contains the gooseberry bush that's planted within. *Meighan Makarchuk*

BELOW: Not all raised beds need to hold veggies. Some simply provide another level of interest in a garden, like this slender version with its eye-catching, tiled sides. *Tara Nolan*

A handmade dibber (a pointed tool used to make holes in the soil for planting seeds) sits on display in Karen Bertelsen's community plot. Bertelsen, who writes the highly entertaining blog *The Art of Doing Stuff,* uses this dibber to create evenly spaced holes for planting in her raised beds. *Karen Bertelsen*

LEFT: A tiered system designed by Ian Wilson of Portland Edible Gardens makes use of an unused corner of a yard. *Ian Wilson*

BELOW: Raised beds don't have to be wide. If they're long and narrow, they're just as accessible to reach into. Here, a raised bed makes use of available space before the yard drops down into a steep slope. *Ian Wilson*

RIGHT: Raised beds come in all shapes and sizes. Here, a gardener has taken advantage of an exceptionally large space and created a big raised bed that's accessible from the inside and outside using a clever shape and pathway. *Steven Biggs*

BELOW: The domino effect: Staggered bricks create great height and an attention-grabbing look for a raised bed. Check local classified ads—you may be able to find someone who wants to unload a pile of bricks! *Steven Biggs*

ABOVE: Colorful hoops have been installed in a few raised beds and remain in place, ready to support a layer of row cover when the weather takes a sudden turn. Row cover can protect plants from frost and high winds, and pests that want to munch on your precious crops.

RIGHT: An old garden gate shows that upcycling is a great way to create various structures for the garden. Here, it's more of a decorative feature, but it can also work as an impromptu trellis in this raised bed. The gate can be pushed into the ground or surrounded by a couple of supports, so that it's sturdy enough to support the weight of a vining plant.

OPPOSITE: Raised beds can be incorporated into the design of your yard so that they blend in more with the landscape. Here, the grass has been kept in place to form a natural pathway between beds. Both edibles and ornamentals have been planted, which make for an eye-catching backyard display.

The height of a raised bed can make all the difference to a gardener who is not able to bend or kneel in a traditional garden.

ABOVE: Adding annual ornamental blooms to a raised bed not only adds a touch of visual interest, it also helps to attract valuable pollinators that can help increase the overall yield of edible plants.

RIGHT: Adding color to raised beds can make for a striking display in the garden, as can a variety of different levels in which you can plant.

ABOVE: Raised beds can be placed on areas with unfavorable growing conditions. Then you get to control the healthy soil that you put in them.

LEFT: The chives lining the raised beds in this English cottage garden prove that edibles can double as ornamentals. They serve as a decorative border while attracting pollinators to the garden and supplying a flavorful garnish.

RIGHT: Patio slabs are another material that makes it easy to create a pathway between raised beds. If you don't have any kicking around your yard, check to see if someone in your area may be getting rid of some.

BELOW: Onions and lettuce make for happy garden companions. Before you plant your veggie garden, do a quick search online to make sure you don't plant any edibles together that won't thrive in each other's presence.

TOP: Wide slabs of wood can be used to make a quick and easy pathway between raised beds.

ABOVE: Search for old cconcrete bricks and stone on sites such as Craigslist to build out the frame of your raised bed. All you might require is a truck to cart them home! *Niki Jabbour*

LEFT: All it takes is one raised bed to grow a sizable harvest that will provide you with fresh meals all season long. *Rich Auger*

Raised beds can also be built out of stacks of new or used bricks. *Tara Nolan*

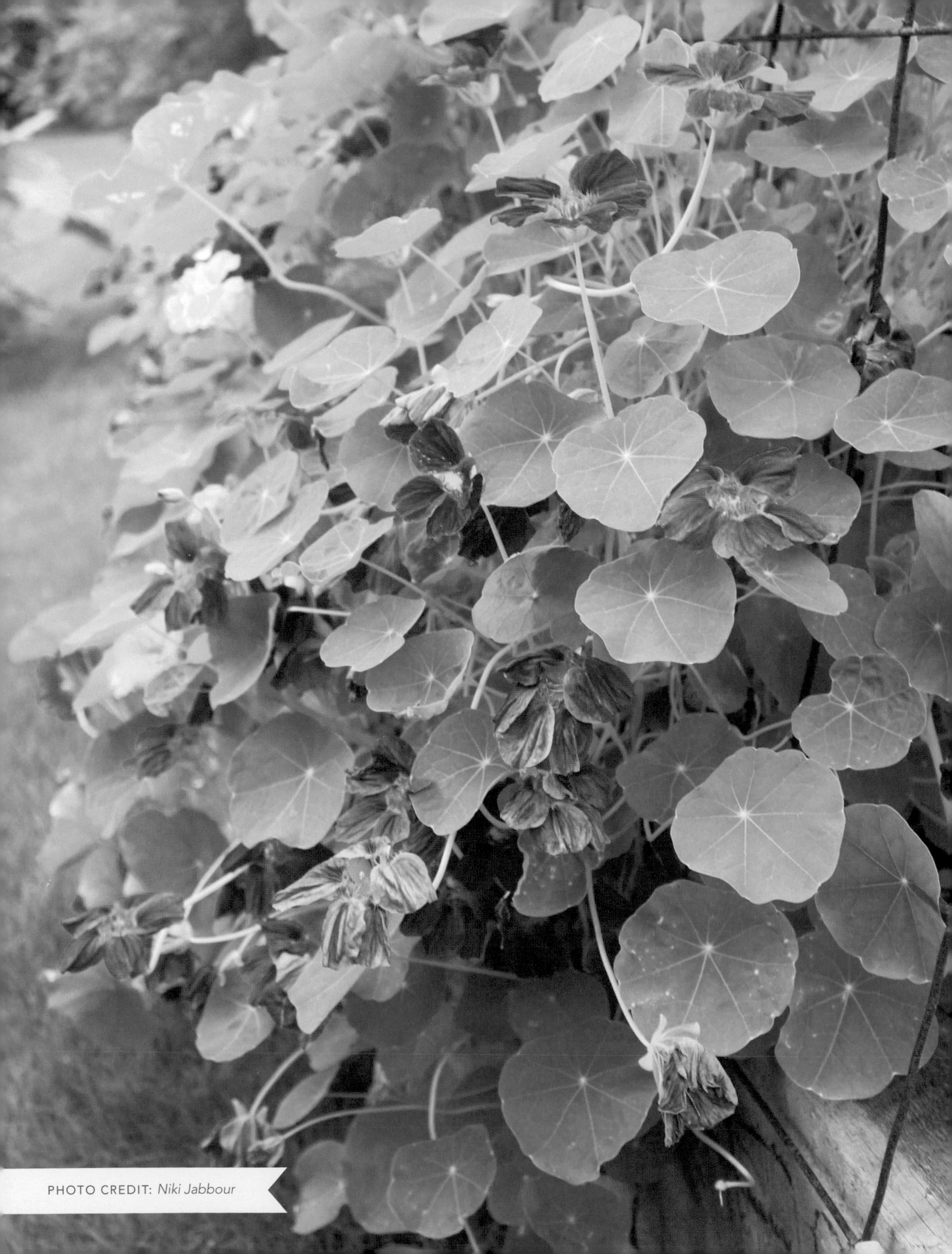

PHOTO CREDIT: *Niki Jabbour*

CHAPTER 2

RAISED BED BASICS

BENEFITS OF RAISED BEDS

There are a multitude of benefits that come from using raised beds, from getting a jump on the growing season to creating ideal growing conditions.

ENJOY AN EARLIER— OR LATER—GROWING SEASON

Depending on the climate where you live, the soil in a raised bed thaws, drains, and warms up sooner in the springtime than the soil in gardens that are in the ground. This means you can get a head start on planting edibles, more specifically cool-weather crops, like peas, lettuce, and beets. You may even be able to plant heat-loving vegetables a little earlier with the help of shelter, such as floating row covers (see page 53) or cloches (small plant covers). Many gardeners don't realize that they can plant and harvest more than one crop during the growing season. Raised beds give you a head start and extend the season beyond the traditional time frame.

A cloche is a valuable raised bed accessory that can protect tender young seedlings from sudden temperature fluctuations in the spring—frost, snow, hail, and so on. It can also protect newly sown seeds from opportunistic squirrels and birds. A cloche basically acts as a

Peas are a great early season crop that you can be enjoying by the time you're ready to plant the heat-lovers, such as peppers and tomatoes. *Jennifer Connell*

ABOVE: Protective cloches can be created out of any clear material, from plastic domes to cocktail glasses. *Niki Jabbour*

BELOW: Special brackets have been added to the side of a raised bed frame to secure the hoops that will support a floating row cover. *Jessica Walliser*

mini protective greenhouse. You can use anything from a traditional cloche to yard sale and antique market finds, like old punch bowls and glasses.

CONTROL PESTS

Depending on the height of a raised bed, you can keep out smaller animals, including rabbits and groundhogs, because they won't be able to climb in. Various barriers can also be installed to prevent rambunctious pet dogs from messing up your garden and to keep out deer that might invite themselves into your yard for a snack.

A variety of materials, such as row cover and hardware cloth, can be added to a raised bed to keep out insects, vermin, and other pests. For example, row cover, added right when you plant your cabbages, can keep away cabbage moths and the cabbage worm eggs they lay. Hardware cloth, installed and secured at the bottom of a raised bed, will prevent moles, voles, and other digging rodents from attacking your crops from underground. You don't want to pull up a fresh beet—or other root vegetable—only to find that a varmint has beaten you to that first bite.

MAKE CROP ROTATION AND COMPANION PLANTING EASY

It's been proven that planting the same thing in the same place year after year is not good for the soil. Raised beds not only make it easy to keep track of what you've planted where each year, they make it easy to move crops around, which helps the fertility of the soil. Rotating crops also aids in preventing pests and diseases.

Companion planting is the method of planting edibles that will thrive and benefit from each other. Many new gardeners don't realize that some edibles simply do not play well together. This could affect your harvest. Cucumbers, for example, do not do well when they're planted in proximity to potatoes, but they will tolerate being

WHAT IS ROW COVER?

Row cover, also referred to as floating row cover, is a lightweight material that can be used to protect crops from a variety of menaces. It allows air and water to permeate so that you don't smother what you're trying to shelter underneath it, and a great deal of light shines through it as well.

Row cover can help protect your newly sown seeds or freshly planted seedlings from marauding squirrels or a strong wind. It can also help speed up the germination rate of seeds.

Ever had a problem with insect pests like cabbage worms? Are birds eating all the ripe berries on your trees or shrubs? Floating row cover is your new best friend.

Depending on the thickness, row cover will also protect your crops from weather fluctuations, ranging from frost to high heat. It can also shield them from the sun's harsh rays.

How to use it: Row cover generally comes in a roll that can easily be trimmed to size with scissors. To protect delicate seedlings, you can add hoops (see Accessorize Your Raised Bed, page 96) to suspend it above the soil. Simply secure it with clamps to the edges of your bed, or use something heavy to hold it down—even tucking all the edges into the soil will do the trick.

Let the pollinators in: While row cover can keep out the bad guys, such as cabbage moths, certain plants such as beans and peas need the good guys—pollinators!—to help those flowers develop into fruit. Once a plant starts to flower, be sure to lift away the row cover so bees and other pollinators can get to work.

planted near nasturtiums, peas, and beans. On the other hand, some plants benefit greatly from being planted together. Basil, for example, is said to improve the flavor of tomatoes.

Planting beans, squash, and corn together is a perfect symbiotic match because sturdy corn stalks act as the perfect trellis up which the nitrogen-rich beans can climb, while the squash spreads outward, choking out any potential weeds.

You can plant groupings of edibles that belong to the same family, such as nightshade veggies—tomatoes, eggplants, and peppers—but sometimes there's an odd man out, like potatoes, which don't thrive around their tomato cousins.

A garden journal can help you keep all of this straight and keep track of what is placed where each season.

PROVIDE ACCESSIBILITY

Raising up the beds makes it easier for those who may have trouble bending over or kneeling down to plant and weed. Some raised bed designs, like the Raised Bed with Benches (see

ABOVE: "The Three Sisters" is a popular label for the classic planting combination of corn, squash, and beans.

BELOW: The Annapolis Royal Historic Gardens feature an Innovative Garden with several accessible raised beds that were designed to be senior- and wheelchair-friendly. *Trish Fry*

WHAT IS AN ENABLING GARDEN?

One amazing benefit of building raised bed gardens is that it gives the opportunity for people of all abilities to enjoy them. Recently, the concept of an "enabling garden" has become popular (and is often linked to horticultural therapy, a type of therapy that uses gardens, landscapes, and plants to improve everything from cognitive to physical well-being). According to a Rutgers Cooperative Extension article: "Enabling Gardens allow participants of all ages and abilities to fully participate and enjoy the gardening experience. They are designed to be barrier-free and to provide sensory stimulation and physical activities in a non-threatening environment."

Features of an enabling garden include being located close to a handicapped-accessible parking lot, minimal slopes and stairs, and wide pathways. Raised beds built according to various requirements, such as being at the proper accessible height for those in wheelchairs, are also helpful additions.

The Guelph Enabling Garden, for example, is a multi-use garden that welcomes anyone to enjoy it, but especially those with physical and cognitive challenges.

Raised beds in a variety of heights for those who wish to either sit or stand are an integral part of the garden that is part of the overall garden's design plan.

There are other enabling gardens across North America that have been created in conjunction with horticultural therapy offerings. They can also be found within retirement and assisted living communities as well as rehabilitation centers.

TOP: The Guelph Arboretum's Enabling Garden has been built to welcome green-thumbed visitors with physical and cognitive challenges.

MIDDLE: Raised beds in an enabling garden may be built at different heights to accommodate the needs of various visitors.

BOTTOM: Concrete pathways make it easy for people using wheelchairs and walkers to navigate around raised beds. *Photos by Jennifer Connell*

page 106), even provide a place to sit. Other designs can be customized to accommodate a wheelchair or scooter.

INCREASE YIELD

Not only will attracting pollinators to your garden boost your harvest, the very act of gardening in a raised bed can be of benefit to your seasonal bounty too. According to an Ohio State University Extension Fact Sheet, a raised bed that was studied over three years at Dawes Arboretum in Newark, Ohio, produced 1.24 pounds of edibles per square foot. That's more than double the yield of what is grown in a conventional garden!

OVERCOME BAD SOIL

The soil conditions of some yards, such as hard-packed clay or excessive sand, might be discouraging to those who want to garden. You can amend these conditions over time, but putting a raised bed over bad soil allows you to bring in your own fresh soil and compost. Essentially you're controlling the environment

of your raised bed. In fact, you don't need to place a raised bed on soil. Raised beds can sit on top of gravel, asphalt, or pavers because it's the soil you add to the beds that is going to be full of the nutrients needed to grow your plants. For example, if your driveway is a prime location because it's the only place that gets six to eight hours of sunshine a day, consider placing your raised bed along the side or across the top—anywhere that will still provide room for your car.

ABOVE: It's not what's underneath the raised bed that counts; it's the soil you put inside. Therefore, this fabric raised bed is perfectly happy resting on patio stones. *Niki Jabbour*

LEFT: Mix in a few ornamental blooms with your edibles to lure beneficial insects into your plot. *Bren Haas*

GARDEN IN LIMITED SPACES

Living in an urban area does not mean having to forsake gardening altogether. There are many compact, creative raised bed alternatives that allow for growing edibles in small, challenging spaces, whether you have a tiny patio, a postage stamp-size lawn, or even a rooftop space or balcony.

KEEP YOUR GARDEN TIDY

Aesthetically, if you have a big space for your crops, raised beds allow you to keep everything neat and orderly. You can connect different beds with pathways lined with mulch or pea gravel, and you don't have to stomp into a growing area to reach the weeds. A great size for raised beds is 3 or 4 feet by 6 feet. This allows you to tend your beds without damaging the soil.

LEFT: Raised beds made from special fabric can be placed on the corner of a deck or balcony, on a small patio, or on a rooftop garden. This one, manufactured by Woolly Pocket, is made from 100 percent recycled materials. *Joshua White*

BELOW: Mulch is an effective way to keep the space around your beds weed-free and tidy. *Ian Wilson*

If you've ever planted mint in your garden, you know by now what a mistake that can be. A fabric raised bed can grow and contain a healthy crop of mint. *Tara Nolan*

ALLOW FOR EASY DRAINAGE

In yards with poor drainage, water may stick around and saturate a traditional garden after a heavy rainfall, harming the roots and promoting mold and disease. By raising up the bed and filling it with healthy, non-compacted soil, you provide a better opportunity for the bed to drain after a heavy rain. You can also add gravel or drainage holes to your beds to provide additional draining capabilities, depending on where your bed is placed.

CONTAIN SPREADERS

Anyone who has ever innocently planted chamomile or mint in the garden and let it go to seed knows what a pain such a plant can be to control. You'll be pulling it out forever! Raised beds can provide a controlled environment that enables you to grow some of the spreaders you know and love but prevent them from taking over the entire garden. (That is, a small raised bed, where you don't plan on planting anything else ever again.) Why Garden in Fabric Pots (see page 245) offers some raised bed recommendations. We've also highlighted an octagonal raised bed that will contain strawberry plants, which are also enthusiastic spreaders (see page 224).

REDUCE WEEDS

You can't help what weed seeds are blown in by the wind, what's dug into the soil by a squirrel, or what's dropped by a bird flying by. Even a soil delivery from a truck can inadvertently introduce a few weed seeds. However, by laying down landscape fabric at the base of your beds, you can smother any nasty weeds that are currently in the ground and prevent them from creeping upward through the soil to invade your bed.

ABOVE: Measure your landscape fabric so that it comes up the sides of the bed, and secure in place with stainless-steel staples. *Donna Griffith*

BELOW: Zinnias from a summer garden make beautiful bouquets. *Jennifer Connell*

GROW A CUTTING GARDEN

From spring through fall, something is always in bloom. What better way is there to celebrate the growing season than with a vase of freshly cut flowers? When you're planting your long-stemmed beauties—cosmos, dahlias, zinnias, coreopsis, gladiolas, and more—in your ornamental gardens, keep a few aside to go into your vegetable raised beds. They'll attract valuable pollinators and beneficial insects to your garden, and you can sacrifice the blooms for container arrangements.

MAKE A TRIAL PLOT

If you're like many a green thumb who comes home from the nursery with more plants than originally intended, raised beds work well as holding areas until you figure out where to plant these extra, unexpected purchases. A corner of a bed can also be reserved for testing out a plant to see how it might perform (before putting it in the garden), to nurse a plant back to health if it hasn't thrived in another area of your yard, or to raise a mystery seedling until you know what it is (and ensure it's not an invasive weed).

PRESERVE YOUR GARDEN SOIL

Tromping through a traditional plot can harm the plants as well as compact the soil. Underneath the soil on the top of a garden is a web of organic activity. Raised beds protect all those vital underground processes, providing you a way to tend the plants without walking on the soil.

In addition, the sides of a raised bed ensure that everything stays in place. In a traditional garden, precipitation has the power to simply wash away your good intentions—and all your healthy soil. And while it's possible that heavy rain can deplete soil in a raised bed (as can a freshly pulled-out crop), it's easy to replenish.

CHOOSING A SIZE

As you will see throughout this book, raised beds come in all shapes and sizes. They're completely customizable depending on the gardener's specific requirements. However, these measurements are considered standard for a typical raised bed.

LENGTH AND WIDTH

The standard length and width of a typical backyard raised bed is about 3 to 4 feet wide by 6 to 8 feet long. This allows for easy access from all sides when you're planting and weeding. It's best to be able to reach into the beds from the side when you're working in them.

Technically, if you want to build one long raised bed, that's narrow in width (because that's what your space allows), you could do that, too, but you must be mindful of the fact that the sides can shift if you don't add supports every few feet.

Staking the side of a raised bed: the ground around your raised bed will shift and heave over time—especially after a rough winter. While it may be tempting to simply create a standard raised bed rectangle with stakes attached to the inside corners, over time you may find the middle of the longest lengths warping out or in, or shifting. One way to avoid this problem is to secure stakes to the outside of the raised bed, about halfway from the end, at the time of building. This should keep the boards firmly in place.

HEIGHT

The height of a raised bed can vary greatly. It might be waist-high or a little bit lower to accommodate a wheelchair, for example. Our raised bed on page 106 has benches installed, perfect for perching as you weed and plant.

Generally, though, raised beds are a bit lower to the ground. A standard rule of thumb is to make them about 10 to 12 inches high. However, if your beds are really low and you're planting

ABOVE: Adding a little reinforcement to the long sides of a raised bed will prevent them from bowing in or out over time. *Donna Griffith*

BELOW: Benches attached to a raised bed provide a comfortable place to rest, but also to garden from. *Donna Griffith*

carrots, parsnips, or other root vegetables, for example, the plants are going to reach down into the subsoil that's beneath the raised bed. If the root vegetables hit the uncompromising soil underneath, they can become stunted and misshapen. Even plants that grow upward will have roots that travel downward, and they may hit the subsoil underneath. If that soil isn't healthy, or it's hard and compacted, it's going to affect the plants. There are measures you can take to amend the subsoil, such as double-digging and adding compost. But if you don't want to have to deal with the subsoil, simply increase the height of the bed a few more inches so your crops will be contained in the raised bed.

If you're upcycling an old container into a raised bed, make sure that the depth will allow for the roots of your chosen plants to flourish. A lettuce table, for example, is very shallow, so it's only suited to plants with equally shallow root systems. Deeper raised beds allow for all other edibles to be planted and to thrive.

SPACING BETWEEN BEDS

The distance between your raised beds is also important. There should be enough space so that you can comfortably bend or kneel down to access the raised beds from the sides. If your raised bed is in a community garden or accessible by the public, you may want to make the spacing even wider to accommodate wheelchairs or walkers. If you'll need to maneuver a wheelbarrow between beds, you'll need to take that into consideration as well.

CHOOSING RAISED BED MATERIALS

Just as the soil you choose is an integral element to creating a raised bed, so are the materials with which you choose to make them.

NEW WOOD

For wooden raised beds, look for untreated, rot-resistant wood. The availability of certain woods at the lumberyard or home improvement center will depend on your location and what grows in your region. However, it's likely that the most common rot-resistant wood you'll find is cedar. Even most of the raised bed kits that you can order online come with cedar boards. Before loading up your cart with wood, be sure to check the price per board so you know how much your raised bed is going to cost. You don't want to be surprised with a budget-busting tab when you get to the checkout.

Look for the Forest Stewardship Council (FSC) stamp when you're purchasing your wood. It's an international certification and labeling system with standards that tracks where your wood has come from and promotes responsible forest management. When you purchase wood with an FSC label, you know it has come from a reputable source and has been properly harvested.

When you're building a bed with rot-resistant wood, the hope is that it will last several years before you have to replace rotting lumber. Some boards will unfortunately age faster than others.

Lining a bed with plastic can help prevent wood from rotting. The lining keeps the wet soil from touching the wood on the inside. Just be sure to only line the sides of the raised bed and not the bottom because the water needs to drain downward and out the bottom of the bed. To avoid rusting, you'll also want to use stainless-steel staples to fasten the plastic or landscape fabric to the bed.

ROT-RESISTANT WOODS

- Black locust
- Black walnut
- Catalpa
- Cedar
- Chestnut
- Cypress

- Hemlock
- Ipé
- Osage orange
- Pressure-treated pine (non-CCA)
- Redwood
- White oak

CEDAR

REDWOOD

PRESSURE-
TREATED
PINE

RECYCLED WOOD

Be careful when you're reusing wood that's come from another project. For example, you want to avoid using railroad ties and pressure-treated wood—especially if you're growing edibles—because the harmful chemicals they were treated with can leach into the soil: Until about 2003 or 2004, chromated copper arsenate (CCA) was used in the making of pressure-treated wood.

Because of past practices, current opinions vary on using the new pressure-treated woods that are on the market. At the time of printing, there is at least one new brand of pressure-treated wood being sold that has environmental certifications. You may want to investigate these materials for yourself and decide what you're comfortable using for your raised beds.

If you're reusing old wood that has an old coat of paint on it, you need to be careful because the paint could contain lead.

TOP: When shopping for wood, look at the end of the board for more details about its origins and treatment. This label, for example, provides information about the type of preservative that was used, and the name and location of the treating company. A quick online search will reveal the answers to any questions you may have about the origins and treatment of certain types of wood.

BOTTOM: Ask an employee at your local lumberyard if you have questions about what the labels on various types of lumber mean, as well as for raised bed wood recommendations.

PROTECTING WOOD

Even if your raised beds are built from rot-resistant wood, they'll still deteriorate over time, and you may need to replace boards here and there. If you want to help prolong the life of your raised beds, you can treat the wood using an eco-friendly stain, although you may still want to confine its use to the outside boards if you're growing food in the bed. Some wood oils use natural ingredients and offer UV protection. Flaxseed oil and wax are natural stains that can be used to protect the wood. Be wary of linseed oil, however; it can contain chemical additives that you don't want around your plants. Do a little research to find a sealer that you feel comfortable using for your raised beds.

ABOVE: Wood preservative can be applied to just about any wood , reclaimed or otherwise, to help it better resist degradation from moisture or insect damage.

BELOW: Choosing multiple paint colors adds a playful element to a raised bed space. *Amy Andrychowicz*

NONWOOD MATERIALS

Some materials will simply last longer than wood. Old paving stones or bricks can be piled to create raised bed walls. Just be mindful of using a technique that ensures they're not going to cave in. As you would with old wood, if you're reusing concrete blocks, for example, be sure you know where they come from. Concrete blocks used to be called "cinder blocks" and were made with fly ash, which is a dangerous substance.

Make sure that whatever material you choose for your raised bed isn't going to leach dangerous chemicals into your soil over time. For example, one safe option is to have a professional weld steel into sturdy raised beds that will truly stand the test of time.

Both new and used stone can be used to frame out a raised bed. *Tara Nolan*

SOIL FOR RAISED BEDS

Now that you've built your raised beds, you need to create a nourishing environment where your plants will grow and thrive.

Healthy, nutrient-rich soil is the number one ingredient to a successful raised bed. Within healthy soil is a web of organic activity created by a variety of microorganisms, such as bacteria, fungi, nematodes, and larger organisms including earthworms. They break down organic matter, leaving behind a trail of nutrients as they move through the soil. Plants absorb these nutrients as they grow and produce blooms and fruit.

You want to encourage and then feed and maintain this little ecosystem, and raised beds are especially helpful in this. One of their benefits is that they allow you to reach into the garden to weed and plant, rather than standing in it and harming these subterranean processes. Many gardeners even subscribe to a no-till method of gardening, meaning they don't disturb the soil at all, ever, once it's been established. They simply add beneficial materials to it and allow nature to work its magic by gradually incorporating the additions into what's already there. This method is also said to promote better aeration and drainage throughout the soil.

Even the United Nations recently acknowledged the importance of healthy soil as it pertains to agriculture and food security by declaring 2015 to be the International Year of Soils. Here's a sample of what was written in the resolution:

> Noting that soils constitute the foundation for agricultural development, essential ecosystem functions and food security and hence are key to sustaining life on Earth,
>
> Recognizing that the sustainability of soils is key to addressing the pressures of a growing population and that recognition, advocacy and support for promoting sustainable management of soils can contribute to healthy soils and thus to a food-secure world and to stable and sustainably used ecosystems.

Be sure to nurture your soil just as you do your plants. Healthy soil = healthy plants.

THE RIGHT SOIL MIX

If you're building one or more larger raised beds for your yard, chances are it's more economical to arrange for soil to be delivered to fill them than buying soil by the bagful. Be careful what kind of soil you order. Topsoil typically won't contain all the wonderful nutrients that you'll find in a special mix, but if that's what you must use, you'll want to heavily amend it with compost or manure. Just be sure to find out where it has come from. A soil delivery company will also likely have different grades of soil, so choose the best one that you can afford. Look for the words "triple mix," which should have a healthy, well-screened mix of topsoil, peat, and compost.

Speaking of triple mix, if you're going to blend your own soil, a good rule of thumb is to mix ⅓ compost with ⅓ peat moss and ⅓ perlite or vermiculite. Mel Bartholomew, who invented the Square Foot Gardening method, recommends that five different types of compost go into that third.

You can also find special blends of container soils mixed specifically for growing edibles. These bags of soil are well-suited to filling a smaller raised bed that's on a balcony, rooftop, or other small space. Keep in mind that there won't be as much organic activity going on in soil that's on a balcony or roof, so it's important to fill your raised bed with the best-quality soil you can afford. You'll want to amend your soil frequently by adding a bit of compost or organic fertilizer to restore any nutrients that are leached out by constant watering.

Amending soil is also important when caring for a raised bed that's on solid ground. A topdressing of compost—about an inch or two—in the spring and fall is usually recommended, but a periodic topdressing throughout the season will work its way into the soil and help to feed it too.

Here are the three key ingredients to a healthy soil:

Compost: Compost is organic matter that has decomposed. Often called "black gold," it adds nutrients to the soil. Compost can come in many forms, from cow manure to a mixture of grass clippings, coffee grounds, and other kitchen waste. You can make your own using a compost bin, buy it in bags, or have it delivered. Compost can be used to amend poor soil, or it can be added to your raised bed soil mix.

Peat moss: Peat moss works on the texture of the soil, allowing it to retain nutrients and water that's slowly delivered to the plants.

Perlite or vermiculite: Both perlite and vermiculite help promote aeration and also work to retain moisture.

What is loam and humus?

Many gardening books and articles refer to having a "loamy" soil. Loam is that perfect balance of sand, silt, and clay in your soil, all ideal components to growing your plants. This is what the plants draw their minerals from. Too much of any of these ingredients, however, like too much clay, can create challenges when you're trying to grow certain plants.

Humus is all that beneficial, organic stuff that's left behind when things like leaves, sticks, and grass clippings break down. It contains a variety of nutrients, including nitrogen, which plants rely on for photosynthesis and growth. When added to your soil—or loam—it provides these nutrients, but it also helps to promote that web of activity mentioned earlier by making the soil more friable. A nice crumbly soil will help promote aeration and water retention as well as provide a nice environment for all those beneficial organisms

WHAT CAN BE ADDED TO A COMPOST PILE?

Making your own compost not only will benefit your garden, it will benefit your wallet. Chances are your household is already discarding the elements that make for a healthy compost.

Here are some elements to add to your compost bin or pile:

YARD DEBRIS
Grass (make sure it's dry)
Leaves (chopping them up will help them break down faster)
Old potting soil
Plants
Soft plant stems

KITCHEN SCRAPS
Coffee grounds with filters
Crushed eggshells
Fruit peels, cores, etc.
Shredded paper
Tea bags (be sure to remove any tags or staples)
Vegetable trimmings

AVOID ADDING THESE ITEMS
Cheese, meat, or other sauces
Dairy products
Fats and oils
Meat, fish, and bones
Metals
Pet waste
Plastics

Locate your compost bin in a sunny area that has good drainage (to promote healthy decomposition and avoid mold). You can make your own bin or purchase one. The manufactured ones are nice for smaller yards where you might not be able to hide a compost bin.

If you don't happen to have the space for a bin, you can purchase compost at a local garden center or soil company. Many municipalities offer free compost in the spring, allowing residents to fill their own bags or containers. Public or botanical gardens may offer this service as well.

TOP: Compost bins come in all shapes and sizes. If you are composting food scraps, enclosed bins with lids can help keep the rodents out.

BOTTOM: Amend the soil in your raised beds with compost in the spring and again in the fall.

that you want to attract so they can get to work in your garden.

Compost is the term used to refer to a manmade decomposition pile. We add our kitchen waste and yard detritus to make our own compost, while humus happens in nature. Essentially, humus is Mother Nature's compost. Both are beneficial to the garden.

HOW MUCH SOIL?

Soil deliveries can be pricey, so you want to make sure that you calculate almost exactly how much soil or compost you'll need (with a little more added as insurance) so you don't need to place another order (and incur another delivery charge). To determine how much soil you need, measure the length, width, and depth of your raised bed and multiply those numbers together to get the amount of cubic feet of soil needed.

There are 27 cubic feet of soil (3 feet × 3 feet × 3 feet) in one cubic yard. To calculate how many cubic yards of soil you'll need, divide the amount of cubic feet by 27.

When you add the soil to your raised bed, fill it until it's almost 2 inches from the top. You'll find that the soil will settle over time. A strong rainstorm may flatten things out as well. You'll also want to replenish the soil whenever you pull out a fresh crop because harvesting can deplete the soil levels. To minimize this, try to shake the soil from the roots of any plants you pull.

If you do happen to order a little too much soil, spread it around your other garden beds, or save it to replenish your raised beds later on in the season.

LOCATION AND SITE MAINTENANCE

CHOOSE THE RIGHT LOCATION

You've decided you want a raised bed. Now, where should you put it? Basically, it needs to go where the most sun is, especially if you're planting edibles. You want your bed to receive at least six to eight hours of sunshine per day.

Before choosing the "forever home" for your raised bed, assess the space you're considering over a couple of days—perhaps over a weekend—and record when the sun hits the space as it moves from east to west. Keep in mind that if you record your sunniest spots in the spring before the leaves have appeared, your chosen area may get a bit more shade throughout the day as the season progresses.

You don't necessarily need an area with grass or soil for raised beds. They can also be placed over hard surfaces such as concrete or pavers.

Try to be a bit strategic when you're planning which direction your raised bed will face. You want to make sure that all the plants in it will enjoy the sunshine. So when you're digging in your seedlings, don't plant the tallest veggies like pole beans or even tomatoes where they're going to cast shade over shorter plants. If there are little spots of shade here and there, you can underplant with veggies that can tolerate shady spots, such as spinach and lettuce.

If your garden is facing the street or you just want it to look tidy from the yard, plant a few ornamentals along the border. Marigolds are good pest preventers, as are nasturtiums (they're edible too!), which will cascade over the sides of your beds as they grow. Other plants like zinnias not only are pretty, they also attract pollinators.

You might also embellish the bed with paint or layers of wood, as we've done with the upcycled bed design on page 100.

ADDING A RAISED BED TO A SLOPE

If your optimal sunny spot happens to be on a slope or uneven stretch of ground, leveling out your raised bed will keep your yard looking neat, and the bed will look as if it's always been there.

3 REASONS WHY YOU SHOULD OWN A COMPOST BIN IF YOU HAVE RAISED BEDS

1. Cut down on household waste. You can divert up to 30 percent of your trash by sending it to the compost bin instead of the garbage can.

2. Create nutrient-rich soil. Your garden will benefit immensely from the "black gold" that you create in your compost bin.

3. Save money. Organic compost can be pricey, so free is even better!

A compost bin is a valuable asset to any garden because it will produce ample amounts of "black gold" all season long—provided that it's regularly filled with organic matter and yard waste. This also benefits your garden budget because you won't have to worry about purchasing the compost from elsewhere.

An easy way to level out your bed—especially if you've built it with stakes in the corners—is to dig in the length that's closest to the slope. Start by putting the lowest corner in the ground and then, using your level, keep measuring the sides as you lift and dig in accordingly. Use soil to shore up the sides or cut pieces to fit bigger spaces that are exposed, and use a stake placed on the inside of the bed to attach it to the whole structure.

PREPPING THE SITE

Lay gravel for drainage
If you're placing your raised bed in an area that doesn't drain well, you may want to place a layer of gravel in the bottom of your bed and even around it so the water can more easily move away from the bed. This will help prevent the bed from rotting and mold from forming. It will also help the soil itself to dry out.

Remove grass from a site
Removing sod isn't an easy task, but you only have to do it once. Mark the area where you want to place your raised bed. Include room for pathways, if you want a delineated space between the grass and your raised bed. Use stakes and string to outline the perimeter where you need to dig. Use an edger or a sharp square spade to cut the sod into easily removable chunks. Some municipalities do not allow discarded sod to be placed in compost bags, so you'll need to figure out where to dispose of it.

The cardboard trick
Digging up grass probably isn't at the top of your landscaping list of tasks because it can be difficult and time-consuming to pick up chunks of sod piece by piece. However, if you plan ahead you can avoid this onerous task by placing cardboard over the area for the raised bed. Then cover the

It may be time-consuming, but you can systematically turn over the sod to make way for raised beds.

cardboard with a layer of soil. The cardboard will kill the grass and break it down, leaving fresh soil in its place. If you do this in the fall, your new garden should be ready by spring. Otherwise, lift up a corner after a few weeks to see if the grass has started to break down. This process also makes it easy to add a pathway. Simply add a layer of landscape fabric to your newly decomposed area and top with the path material of choice, such as pea gravel, straw, or mulch.

TIPS FOR DEALING WITH SLOPES

The following tips for dealing with a slope are from Ian Wilson of Portland Edible Gardens. If you have a sloped area that happens to be exactly where you want to place your raised bed, there are a few things you can do to accommodate a new garden. *Photos by Ian Wilson*

RIGHT: In cases that require or recommend building down the contour, it's often helpful to terrace or step raised beds incrementally to account for the slope. This method, though more involved, makes for an elegant and aesthetic design.

BELOW: Building raised garden beds on slopes is always challenging. The easiest approach is always to orient raised beds along the contour of the slope. This requires the least amount of excavation and grading of the terrain prior to installation.

RAISED BED MAINTENANCE

Over time, harsh winters and general wear and tear can cause your beds to heave, resulting in uneven boards. Even rot-resistant wood will break down over time. Check your raised beds in the springtime for rot, and replace any deteriorated boards that are easy to disassemble from the frame with new boards.

You also should check for any boards that bow out. You may have seen raised beds with stakes along the longest sides. They can be unsightly, but they really help hold the boards in place. To add a stake, drive it into the ground about halfway along the outside of the frame. (See Essential Raised Bed, page 88, for an example.)

Feed the soil

Continuous watering of your raised beds throughout the season naturally leaches the nutrients out of the soil. In addition, the plants are also absorbing nutrients from the soil and using them to grow. As a result, you need to regularly give your soil a little boost, either by adding an organic fertilizer such as kelp or by spreading fresh compost on the top of the soil.

Rotate crops

One of the benefits of having multiple raised beds is that you can easily move your crops around from bed to bed each year. This is called "crop rotation." Farmers use this method to manage the fertility of the soil in their fields. Continuously planting the same crop heavily depletes the soil. Even in a home garden, crop rotation is important for a variety of reasons—it helps to minimize soilborne diseases and pests, and it helps you manage the nutrient levels and fertility of the soil. Try to move different families of vegetables around.

PREPARE BEDS FOR WINTER

As you complete your autumn gardening tasks throughout your entire yard, there are a few things you can do to tuck in your raised beds for winter.

- Once you've pulled out and composted all the spent plants, add a few inches of compost to replenish the beds.

- Keep your leaves! Leaf mold is a great soil amendment ingredient. If you have the space, keep a pile where they can break down over time. Or if you want to use some leaves right away, run over them a few times with a lawnmower to break them up, and then add a layer of them to your raised bed. The earthworms will love you.

  Don't, however, add a big pile of large leaves to the garden. They can become moldy and smother the soil rather than enhance it. If you notice any diseased leaves, be careful not to add those to your soil. And don't use leaves from a black walnut tree. They contain juglone, a toxic chemical that many plants do not like.

- If you've planted garlic or cool-weather root crops that you'll be harvesting throughout the winter, lay down a layer of straw (not hay, because of the seeds) to keep things nice and cozy.

- Remove any plant supports, trellises, or garden ornaments, clean the soil off of them with an old cloth, and store them.

- If you have removable row cover hoops, you may want to install them in the raised bed and keep the row cover close at hand. That way, if there's a sudden frost warning, you can run outside and cover up any crops that need protection.

- Keep a small shovel or brush handy to brush snow off cold frames or row cover.

- For balcony beds, remove and discard the soil completely so that you can start fresh in the spring. The freeze and thaw cycles of the winter can wreak havoc on smaller beds, causing the wood to heave or crack.

PLANT COVER CROPS

A cover crop is a crop that's planted to help replenish and improve the soil between plantings. For example, once garlic or any cool-weather crop is harvested (often in mid-summer), there's an empty space left in the garden. Cover crops can be planted there. They're fast-growing and return nutrients to the soil once you dig them under. That's why they're also referred to as "green manure" because essentially you're growing your compost.

Buckwheat is a popular mid-season cover crop. It matures within 70 to 90 days, helps to keep the weeds down, and attracts beneficial insects to the garden. Just be sure to turn it under before the seeds form.

Fall is a great time to grow cover crops because you've reaped most, if not all, of your harvest and the beds are just laying bare, waiting for spring. Peas and clover work well because they add lots of nitrogen back into the soil. Winter wheat and winter rye are also popular choices that can be planted in fall and dug into the soil a few weeks before you want to plant your first spring crop.

KEEP CONSTRUCTION TO A MINIMUM

If you don't consider yourself particularly handy, specially made corners allow for a quick and easy raised bed setup. Simply lay out your wood cut to the lengths that you want as well as the decorative corners that you've purchased, slide everything in place, and fasten it all together (see page 242). Make sure each side is level as you position the bed where you want it.

A few packages of corners can allow you to create an instant collection of raised beds with a minimal amount of work. *Gardener's Supply Company*

A NOTE TO NEW GARDENERS WHO HAVE INSTALLED THEIR FIRST RAISED BED

If your shiny new raised bed is your first foray into gardening, fear not. There are ample online resources that can help a newbie gardener figure out what to plant—or troubleshoot any problems that may arise throughout the growing season.

To help you figure out what seeds to sow or which seedlings to buy at the garden center, think about the items that regularly make it onto your grocery list. Fresh herbs are some of the easiest plants to grow. And they can cost big bucks for a small bunch in the produce aisle. If you love tomatoes, then pick three to five plants that include a nice large slicing tomato and a snack-worthy cherry variety.

Peas, beans, and cucumbers are also relatively easy to grow and yield a sizable harvest; just be sure to give them something to climb.

Even the most experienced gardeners learn through trial and error, so don't be afraid to make mistakes! There's always next year.

Plant the things that most often find themselves in your shopping cart. © *Les Urbainculteurs / Smart Pots*

SOLUTIONS FOR RAISED BED ROADBLOCKS

Are there certain limitations holding you back from building a raised bed? Do you lack the necessary tools or skills? Here are some ideas that can help you turn your raised bed aspirations into a reality.

Let someone else do the prep work. Have all your lumber precut where you purchase it, so all you have to worry about is assembly when you get home. Many home centers and some lumberyards offer this service.

Have your materials delivered. If your raised bed materials won't fit in your small car, or if you're limited to public transportation, have them delivered. Better yet, purchase a kit online and receive everything you'll need ready-to-assemble and delivered right to your doorstep.

Borrow or rent tools. If you aspire to build things, but you simply don't own the tools, see if you can borrow them from a friend or neighbor, or rent them. Many

home centers feature rental departments where you can pay to reserve and sign out tools for a day or more. Some communities even offer tool libraries where, for a nominal membership fee, you can sign out various tools just as you would a book at the library.

Use what you've got. Not ready to shell out for raised bed materials? Test out your commitment to having a raised bed by raiding your shed, attic, basement, or backyard for items that you can repurpose, such as old washtubs, dressers, or wine crates.

BELOW: This washbasin, discovered at an antique market, was turned into a raised bed for root veggies and greens. *Tara Nolan*

OPPOSITE: If something is preventing you from building a raised bed, improvise by borrowing tools or arranging for material delivery, etc. *Niki Jabbour*

CONSIDER DRIP IRRIGATION

There are several ways you can give thirsty plants in your raised beds a drink. You could simply fill a watering can and lug it from bed to bed, watering the base of the plants and trying to avoid getting the leaves wet (when water splashes up from the soil and touches the leaves, it can spread diseases to the plant).

Or you can just bring your hose to the beds and water that way—again, gently, at the base of the plants.

But there's a better way to water that requires less effort—it just takes a bit of planning and installation work: drip irrigation.

Drip irrigation is a common method used to water raised beds. It can be installed by a professional or by a keen DIYer. Drip irrigation kits are readily available for purchase at home improvement stores and nurseries. They guide you through the entire installation process and generally come with all the basic parts you'll need to put together a system. There are also add-ons you can purchase later to put your system on a timer or distribute fertilizer.

Drip irrigation is not only efficient, it's a great way to conserve water because it delivers it directly to the root zone of the plants, so no water is lost to evaporation. You're also not watering the weeds. A drip hose is generally looped around the perimeter of the garden and up the middle rows, depending on the width of the garden. You can also have lines going from garden to garden or from pot to pot. The water gently trickles out of what is called an "emitter." Different types of emitters distribute water at different rates (gallons per minute or gallons per hour).

DIY KITS

You'll typically find the following components in a DIY drip irrigation kit:

- A Y-shaped connector that connects to the outside faucet. It allows water on one side to feed your regular hose and water on the other side to feed your irrigation system.

- At the very end of the hose, there is a plug, which prevents water from flowing out the end (you only want it to flow out the emitters).

- A pressure regulator to maintain a consistent water pressure.

- A backflow preventer to ensure that nothing is sucked from the garden hose back into your water supply.

- Connectors that allow you to direct irrigation in multiple directions in the garden.

- Tubing or hose that transports the water to the garden.

- Various emitters that release water to the plants a bit differently. They can be referred to as bubblers and xeri emitters. Both emit fine sprays but at different rates. These types of emitters will lose water through wind and evaporation, but they do work around shrubs and trees and in containers.

These are components that are often offered as optional add-ons:

- A drip irrigation standard tubing hole punch allows you to attach a drip line connector to your main hose.

- Timers let you program the start and stop time automatically at the time of day you set it to. They're especially handy if you're away from home frequently.

- Special sensors determine if it's rained and can cancel a timed watering if the soil hasn't yet dried out.

- A fertilizer injector sends nutrients through the tubing to your plants.

OPPOSITE: Driplines running through a raised bed distribute water evenly to the roots. *Ian Wilson*

RIGHT: An irrigation system is used to water these potted peppers, which are located in a hot, sunny area along the side of blogger Amy Andrychowicz's house. Each pot is fitted with its own drip head, an adjustable dripper on a stake, so that the pepper plants can be regularly watered without having to go from pot to pot with the hose or a watering can. This system could easily be applied to a raised bed. *Amy Andrychowicz*

BELOW: This garden kit has 10 drippers with a 24-inch hose and connectors. The setup is easily customizable and works as a network with any standalone water supply, such as a bucket, garbage bin, or rain barrel. *© Les Urbainculteurs/Smart Pots*

RIGHT: Michael Holmes, the gardener who planted the bush beans in these half barrels, has invented his own mini irrigation system. A layer of mulch is spread along the bottom (you could also use Styrofoam peanuts or gravel). He then adds a growing medium, which is a lightweight mix of black earth, loam, and some sand, as well as manure and blood or bone meal for long-term nitrogen. A piece of plastic pipe is placed into the barrel so that the water can get down to the bottom. The bean seedlings are planted with a couple of inches of mulch on top of the soil. Holmes checks that the soil is moist and adjusts the amount of water he adds daily according to the plant's growth as well as the heat and sun. As much as 2 gallons of water are added at the peak of production. Plants are also fed with a weekly dose of water-soluble fertilizer. *Donna Griffith*

BELOW: A plethora of fabric raised beds are gathered on the roof of this convention center. You can see the drip irrigation lines that run from pot to pot to ensure plants are well hydrated. © *Les Urbainculteurs/Smart Pots*

THE BENEFITS OF MULCH

Not only does mulch suppress weeds, it prevents water evaporation and helps soil retain moisture, which means you don't have to water as often. Common mulches include straw, shredded cedar, pine bark, and even compost made from grass clippings, decomposed leaves, and other garden debris.

A layer of straw mulch can keep weeds at bay. It also helps to retain moisture. *Bren Haas*

TIPS FROM A DRIP IRRIGATION EXPERT

Brandon Park is the owner of Urban Irrigation Solutions, a company that installs irrigation systems. He says there are a lot of innovative DIY irrigation solutions on the horizon. The trend is moving toward water conservation technologies and better design.

- For raised beds, Park lays driplines on the root system, which he says results in almost zero water loss.

- For new plants that aren't that well established, Park recommends watering every day for about two to three weeks. Once the plants are established, he recommends watering three days a week. The trick is to water plants deeply but less frequently. A heavy soak will provide ample water to the root system and watering less frequently gives it time to dry out before the next soak.

- Every system Park installs has a timer that's set by him or the homeowner to water the raised beds at specific times. Park recommends watering between 5:00 and 7:00 a.m. If you water at night, he warns, the water sits there and creates an environment for fungus and bacteria to grow. If you water too late in the morning, you'll lose water to evaporation.

- The type of soil you have is also a big indicator of how frequently you should water, though raised beds that have premium soil should drain well when watered.

- Constant watering throughout the season is naturally going to deplete your soil of nutrients. If you're watering every day, Park recommends fertilizing by adding a fresh layer of soil or manure to your raised beds.

- Park installs a rain sensor for every system, which prevents the garden from being watered when it's not needed.

- While there are DIY irrigation kits, Park says it does take some forethought to design an irrigation system. There is a mathematical formula that determines the size of the pipes needed to ensure water uniformity and pressure. He recommends a homeowner look online for a formula to determine the pressure loss so that everything runs smoothly once it's connected.

- For rooftops, the same systems are used, but the roof must be checked to make sure it has a good water barrier and proper drainage.

- For bigger jobs, an architect will be consulted to check the building's blueprints and make sure the roof is capable of handling soil and the weight of the water.

Concealing drip irrigation

It's easiest to conceal hoses and a dripline when the raised beds aren't too far from the hose. Mulch is a good irrigation system cover because it's lightweight and readily available.

Of course, installing an irrigation system sometimes requires digging to run the hoses under a path or section of lawn. This can be done by installing conduit pipe and then running the hose through it to where it needs to go.

Check hoses regularly

You'll need to regularly look over your hoses carefully for leaks and for plugged emitters that might have debris in them that prevent the water from coming out where it should.

LEFT: This irrigation system installed in a raised bed is ready for plants. *Brandon Park*

BELOW: An irrigation system is a great way to conserve water, especially when there are multiple beds that need a daily soak. *Steven Biggs*

INSTALL A RAIN BARREL

Any time you can avoid turning on your outdoor tap to water, you're saving money. A good rainstorm helps give crops a thorough soaking. And a rain barrel is a cost-saving way to collect the rainwater that would otherwise drain into the yard. Rain barrels are easy to install and require minimal maintenance. They have special nets that ensure that mosquitoes, who are attracted to standing water, don't breed in them. And all rain barrels have a spigot, but you can also hook up a hose to water your yard.

ABOVE: A rain barrel diverts and stores water from your downspout.

LEFT: Creating a notch in the side of a raised bed can help to guide an irrigation line into the garden and keep it in place. *Jessica Walliser*

HOW DO YOU KNOW IF YOU'VE OVERWATERED?

Obviously we can't help how much rain Mother Nature decides to give to our plants, but we can control how much we water them. Many plants don't like to be overwatered and will start to show signs of distress if they're getting waterlogged. The soil should dry out completely between watering. Test for moisture by inserting your finger a couple of inches into the soil to see if it feels damp. If it does, don't water. Signs of overwatering include a plant that's wilted and/or has yellow leaves.

CHAPTER 3

RAISED BEDS FOR BIG SPACES

If you have a yard, you're in luck. You can build one—or two or three or even more—raised beds. You have so many options for different shapes, heights, and sizes. You can experiment with crop rotation. You can add pathways and trellis systems and irrigation. Nowadays, with the popularity of edible gardening, the choices are endless. There are multiple benefits to growing edibles in raised beds, which have been outlined throughout this book. The first project for this chapter is a plan for what is referred to as the essential raised bed. There are a few different ways to make a raised bed, but this plan in particular has been created to facilitate the addition of various accessories. Because not only are there various design options, there are also many add-ons you can introduce to help you even further with your harvest—pest prevention, staking and trellis systems, frost protection, and more.

Front yard veggie gardens are also becoming more prominent as homeowners eschew the typical expanse of grass for something more practical. Often that's simply where the most sunlight happens to be. So, if your tomatoes are going to ripen in the front and flounder in the back, consider raised beds in your front yard—just be sure to consult your municipality's bylaws before you get started.

If you want to jazz up a raised bed, whether it's visible to the public from the front or side of the house, or you want to add character to the back, there are a few things you can do, including adding a coat of paint or recreating a similar puzzle-like pattern using old pieces of wood in varying hues and thicknesses, as has been done for the upcycled project that can also be found in this chapter (see page 100).

While a raised bed with benches provides a useful, accessible design, setting a pond into a raised bed is an example of taking one's imagination beyond the standard planting scheme.

For further inspiration, you may discover that many community garden plots have adopted the neat and tidy aesthetic of raised beds. Botanical gardens and other public spaces dedicated to growing food can also be great sources of ideas.

THE ESSENTIAL RAISED BED

Design adapted by Scott McKinnon
Photography by Donna Griffith
Illustration by Len Churchill

Raised beds are popping up everywhere, from botanical gardens and backyards to community gardens and rooftops. Green thumbs all over the world are hopping on the raised bed bandwagon because they make gardening so darned easy and they look good.

If your beds are going in the backyard—or a community garden space—then you might be content with a typical, easy-to-construct design. There are a few easy ways to make your standard, rectangular raised bed. One is simply to stack timber, tailored to the width and length of your space, staggering the corner joints and securing with 6-inch nails driven down from each top corner through ³⁄₁₆-inch pilot holes. Another way is to cut two 8-foot 1-inch by 6-inch boards in half for the ends, and use four 1 by 6-inch boards for the two longer sides, stacking them two high and attaching everything with outdoor screws to four by four posts positioned on the inside corners. Be sure to leave a few inches on the ends of the posts to anchor the raised beds firmly into the ground. (And refer to step 6 for an important tip about reinforcing the sides.)

One big advantage of planting in raised beds is the ability to shelter your edibles from menaces to your plants, such as pests (destructive insects, bunnies, birds) or inclement weather (frost, high winds). This project in particular features a wooden edge—or rail—that frames the top of the raised bed structure, making it easy to secure with spring clamps, row cover, plastic, or netting over PVC hoops (see Accessorize Your Raised Bed, page 96, for step-by-step instructions). The curved shape created by PVC pipe mimics the outline of a hoop house, a structure that farmers use to protect their crops. Here, we're just doing it on a smaller scale. Another bonus? The PVC structure is easy to take apart and store over the winter months!

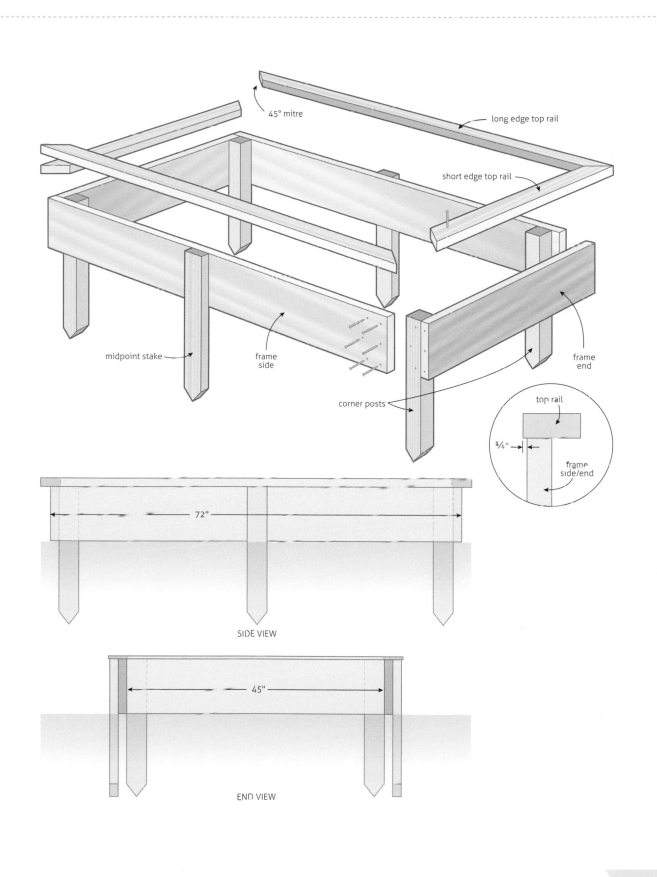

45° mitre

long edge top rail

short edge top rail

midpoint stake

frame side

frame end

corner posts

top rail

1/4"

frame side/end

72"

SIDE VIEW

45"

END VIEW

Tools

- Tape measure
- Hammer
- Circular saw
- Carpenter's square
- Rubber mallet or hand sledgehammer
- Level
- Reciprocating saw or handsaw
- Drill with countersink bit and $\frac{3}{16}$" twist bit
- Eye and ear protection
- Work gloves

Materials

- $3\frac{1}{2}$" and $1\frac{1}{4}$" deck screws
- (2) 2 × 10" ×10'
- (1) 4 × 4" × 8' (or 2 × 4") (for stakes)
- (3) 2 × 4 × 8'
- (1) 2 × 2" or use scrap from a 2 × 4" sawn in half

Cut list

PART	DIMENSION	PCS
Frame, side pieces	$1\frac{1}{2} \times 9\frac{1}{4} \times 45$"	2
Frame, long pieces	$1\frac{1}{2} \times 9\frac{1}{4} \times 72$"	2
Corner posts	$3\frac{1}{2} \times 3\frac{1}{2} \times 24$"	4
Top rails, long sides (from 45° mitered ends)	$1\frac{1}{2} \times 3\frac{1}{2} \times 68\frac{1}{2}$"	2
Top rails, short sides (from 45° mitered ends)	$1\frac{1}{2} \times 3\frac{1}{2} \times 44\frac{1}{2}$"	2
Stakes	$1\frac{1}{2} \times 1\frac{1}{2} \times 12$"	2

HOW TO MAKE THE
ESSENTIAL RAISED BED

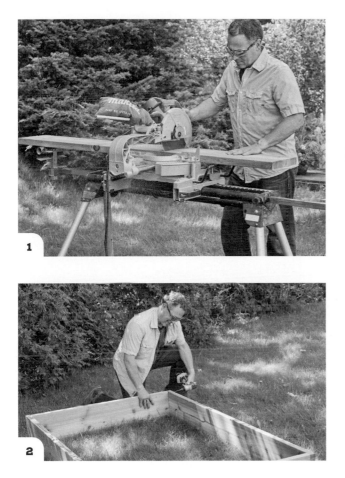

STEP 1: CUT PIECES TO SIZE.

With a circular saw, cut a 45-inch and a 72-inch piece out of each 2 × 10-inch × 10-foot board. Use a carpenter's square to make sure the cuts are straight and at 90 degrees. These are your frame pieces.

STEP 2: CREATE THE FRAME.

Line up the side pieces on the outside of the ends (the shorter pieces inside the longer ones). Make sure everything is flush, and drill three evenly spaced pilot holes through the sides and end pieces at each corner. Use 3½-inch deck screws to fasten everything together.

STEP 3: MAKE THE CORNER POSTS.

Cut the 4 × 4-inch × 8-foot board equally into four pieces (about 24 inches each). Trim the ends of each post into a point, using a reciprocating saw or handsaw. This will make it easier to drive them into the ground.

STEP 4: POSITION THE FRAME.

Remove any grass or weeds that will end up beneath your raised bed. Make sure the ground is level. Once you're ready, place the raised bed frame in its final destination. Measure diagonally between the opposing corners to ensure the bed is square. Measurements should be equal on both diagonals.

STEP 5: SECURE THE FRAME.

In each inside corner, position the corner posts and use a mallet or hand sledge and a wood block to drive the post into the ground. The tops should be about 2 inches below the top of the bed frame. Check that the frame is sitting level. Once it's in place, drill pilot holes from the outside into the post and secure with 3½-inch deck screws.

STEP 6: REINFORCE THE MIDPOINT.

Using a mallet, strike a 2 × 4 stake firmly into the ground on the outside of the bed frame at the midpoint. Do this for each long side (don't worry about the ends), and secure with a couple of screws. You could also use rebar. This is an important step; it will prevent the lumber from shifting over time.

STEP 7: INSTALL THE TOP RAIL.

Out of an 8-foot board, cut a 45-degree miter close to one end. Measure 68½ inches from the shorter end of the miter, and cut an opposing miter at that point. Repeat with a second 8-foot piece.

Out of the remaining piece, cut two pieces the same way but 44½ inches between the miters.

Secure with 1¼-inch screws, making sure that there's an even overlap all around. The boards should overlap the inside edge of the frame walls by ¼ inch all around.

PLANT IT!

Arriving at your local garden center can be extremely overwhelming—especially if you go without a list. Your first visit may simply be a reconnaissance mission where you scope out what's available. Then when you get home, you can figure out what to plant in your raised bed. Essentially, you want to plant your grocery list, with tried-and-true family favorites and a few new-to-you edibles planted somewhere in the mix.

Think about the foods that you frequently use when cooking. Are you constantly throwing a packet of fresh herbs in your cart? Those add up; it's much cheaper to buy one plant and snip it throughout the season. If it's an herb you really like, buy a backup plant—or two—just in case you give one plant too much of a haircut.

Keep in mind that side dish mainstays, like carrots and potatoes, can be stored over the winter months. And an overabundance of cucumbers can keep you in pickles until spring.

What do you generally toss into a salad? Add to your list green onions, tomatoes, and a variety of greens, from lettuces to kale and mustard.

The key is to plant a variety of food that your family will enjoy throughout the harvest season—and, if you think ahead, until the end of the winter.

PLANT NEW-TO-YOU
EDIBLES IN YOUR RAISED BED

Besides your dependable list of edibles that you enjoy, try to add at least one that's new to you each season. It's fun to discover new flavors for meals and preserving. And it's entertaining to serve uncommon-looking edibles and explain to your guests what they are. Here are a few that you may encounter as you flip through seed catalogs.

Lemongrass, which looks like a dracaena, can usually be found among the herbs. Its fragrant stalks can be used in everything from herbal tea to Thai cooking.

ABOVE, LEFT: Cucamelons: Also referred to as Mexican sour gherkins and mouse melons, these little gems that are about as long as a quarter look like tiny watermelons. But they taste more like a tart cucumber. *Tara Nolan*

LEFT: Colorful heirlooms: Keep an eye out for common edibles in uncommon colors, such as yellow beets, pink tomatoes, or purple carrots. *Tara Nolan*

BELOW: Lemon cucumbers: These guys look a bit threatening when you first pick them—they're covered in little spikes. However, they can easily be brushed off, and what you'll find inside is a delicious-tasting cucumber. *Niki Jabbour*

ACCESSORIZE YOUR
RAISED BED

So you've built a basic raised bed. What now? Just like a car, raised beds aren't one-size-fits-all. Some gardeners may need a few extra features, like pest preventers or season extenders, while others will benefit from some helpful modifications such as extra drainage allowances. Here are a few ideas that you can use to customize your own raised bed.

LINE YOUR BED WITH LANDSCAPE FABRIC.

Depending on where you place your new raised bed, lining the bottom with landscape fabric will prevent weeds from growing up into your pristine soil. It can be found by the roll at home improvement centers and hardware stores. The fabric is permeable, so water drains through it. It's also a great material to lay under the pathways of gravel or mulch that you may create between your raised beds to thwart weeds.

To make it easier to toss the new soil into the bed, you may want to first secure the landscape cloth to the bottom sides of your raised bed using stainless-steel staples. *Donna Griffith*

KEEP VOLES AND MOLES OUT WITH HARDWARE CLOTH.

The term *hardware cloth* can be a bit deceiving because this material is not made of fabric. In fact, it's more of a sturdy wire mesh—like chicken wire, but with smaller holes—that will keep digging rodents, such as moles, voles, and gophers, from coming up into your beds to eat your harvest from below. Lay the hardware cloth at the bottom of a raised bed before you add the landscape fabric. Be sure to wear gloves for this task because the ends are very sharp. Use tin snips to cut a piece to size, and make sure you secure it firmly at the bottom of the bed with stainless-steel staples. *Andrea Hungerford*

DETER SLUGS WITH COPPER TAPE.

If slugs happen to be a problem in the garden, there are copper slug tapes on the market that are meant to repel them. Copper is said to contain a small electrical charge that keeps slugs and snails from crossing over it. Place it around a raised bed and challenge those annoying insects to dare to come to the other side. *Donna Griffith*

ADD A LAYER OF MULCH TO YOUR BEDS.

There are several benefits to laying mulch over the soil in your raised beds. Mulch helps keep the soil cool on especially hot days and also helps the plants to retain water. Popular mulch materials include straw (not hay because of the seeds). As it breaks down, mulch can also add nutrients back into the soil. Just be sure to keep the mulch from touching the stems of your plants to allow them to breathe and to prevent disease.

TURN YOUR RAISED BED INTO A MINI HOOP HOUSE.

Start your season early or extend it well into fall by covering your raised bed with row cover. Row cover comes in different weights depending on the season in which you use it. It can help protect your crops from the elements and pests.

Tools

- Utility knife blade or PEX pipe cutter
- 6 to 12 spring clamps
- Eye protection
- Work gloves

Materials

- ½" PEX pipe (5 pieces cut to 75")
- Plastic or row cover (8 × 14')
- (10) ½" PVC conduit clamps

STEP 1: Attach ½" PVC conduit clamps with screws every few inches along the length of your raised bed on the inside (in this case, they're screwed to the top rail, as shown in the Essential Raised Bed plan, page 88). Make sure they're the same distance apart on both sides so the PEX hoops line up.

Cut your lengths of PEX pipe using a utility knife blade or PEX pipe cutter. *Donna Griffith*

STEP 2: Bend and place the PEX through the clamps on each side to form a hoop shape. *Donna Griffith*

Note: If you're concerned about snow load, you may want to create a spine from another length of PEX that's attached down the middle of your hoops. Attach this with 1¾-inch #8 stainless-steel machine bolts and wingnuts (for easy disassembly).

STEP 3: When you're ready to add a row cover, netting, or plastic, drape the material over the cover frame, centering it from side to side and end to end. Use the clamps to attach the material to the rail so it doesn't blow away. To prevent plastic covers from overheating your crops, you can roll up the ends and clamp the material to the outside ribs to let the air flow through. *Tara Nolan*

INSTALL STAKES AND TRELLISES.

It's very important to stake plants to keep leaves and stems from touching the ground (which can encourage disease) and from crowding out other plants in the garden. Try to add any cages, stakes, or trellises close to the time of planting because stems can inadvertently be snapped if you try to add them later to a more mature plant. Staking plants also frees up space in the garden for other plants. If climbers head upward, all of a sudden you have new real estate.

If you need to tie stems and branches to a stake, use a gentle material, like a Velcro plant tie, so that you don't inadvertently harm the plant. *Brenda Franklin*

KEEP PETS AWAY FROM YOUR CROPS.

Avoid over-exuberant dogs from leaping into your raised beds and digging by adding stakes to the corners and tying string around the perimeter a couple of times. The string in this raised bed deters two sheepdogs from leaping in and snatching the produce. Cats are a little more wily, so they're going to find a way in no matter what. *Donna Griffith*

DEER-PROOF YOUR BED.

Deer are a little harder to deter than smaller animals, but there are ways to keep them out of your raised beds. The structures are just built on a larger scale. Fencing in an area at a height where the deer cannot leap over will help, but you can also create fencing that simply fits over a raised bed. Some gardeners also cover the top of a raised bed with fencing, and simply lift off the "lid" when they want to get into the garden. *Meighan Makarchuk*

INSTALL AN IRRIGATION SYSTEM.

If you travel or you're away from your garden frequently, an irrigation system will keep the plants in your raised beds well hydrated so you can still come home to a healthy crop—and hopefully edibles that are ready to harvest. (See Chapter 2, page 79, for more information.) *Hilary Dahl for Seattle Urban Farm Co.*

MEASURE PRECIPITATION WITH A RAIN GAUGE.

Add up the amount of rain that's fallen over the season by placing a rain gauge in your garden bed. Check and empty it every week or so, and record how many millimeters have fallen. A rain gauge will also help you determine if a recent rainfall provided enough of a drink for your plants. *Tara Nolan*

ADD DRAINAGE.

It's important that your raised beds drain well so that the roots of the plants are able to dry out between watering and to prevent them from drowning in water that won't drain. If you're placing your raised bed in an area of the yard that does not tend to dry out after heavy watering, you can add a layer of crushed gravel to the bottom before you add in the soil. Some beds also can benefit from weep holes, which are holes drilled upward through the sides of the bed that allow water to drain.

PROVIDE A PLACE FOR POLLINATORS.

Important insects will be visiting your garden to pollinate your plants. Some will even take care of the bad guys! Besides planting for pollinators, you can also provide important elements that will keep them around. For example, birdbaths and water bowls provide a place for them to drink; carefully placed solitary bee houses can provide shelter. *Johanne Daoust*

MEASURE TEMPERATURES WITH AN INDOOR/OUTDOOR THERMOMETER.

Believe it or not, even in the dead of winter, the solar energy captured by a cold frame can make it too hot inside for your plants. A min/max thermometer will help you determine whether or not you need to vent your cold frame (which is done simply by opening the lid and using a sturdy stake to keep it lifted). Keep in mind that with the lid closed, you don't want the temperatures inside to rise above 60 °Fahrenheit during the day. *Tara Nolan*

INSTALL A HEAT-ACTIVATED WINDOW OPENER.

An automatic window opener is a great gadget for a cold frame or a greenhouse—especially if you happen to find yourself away from home for a few days. A suddenly warm, sunny day can wreak havoc on tender leaves in a cold frame, essentially cooking them in the garden and ruining your crop. Venting both a cold frame and a greenhouse when the temperatures fluctuate is integral to the health of the plants. An opener has a sensor that will expand when venting needs to occur, automatically pushing the window—or whatever it's attached to—open for you. And it will contract once the temperature has dipped once again.

RAISED BED WITH UPCYCLED WOOD

Designed by Scott McKinnon
Photography by Donna Griffith
Illustration by Len Churchill

This project design takes the standard raised bed to a whole new level. Old strips of wood in varying grains, colors, and thicknesses have been used to create an eye-catching garden. Let's call it rustic-chic.

The snazzy raised bed shown here was built for the side yard of a corner lot and has attracted many appreciative glances from the neighbors and dog walkers who happen by. It also happens to be in a prime, sunny spot where veggies don't just thrive, they're almost busting out of the bed! Besides using good-quality soil, where you place your bed is one of the key ingredients to reaping a bountiful harvest. You want to make sure the space you choose sees at least six to eight hours of sun a day, especially if you're planting heat-loving edibles like peppers and tomatoes.

To create the look, strips of wood are sourced from a variety of different places and cut to different lengths. These strips are then carefully pieced over panels made from cedar fence boards. They kind of act like a protective barrier, potentially prolonging the life of your bed. This effect could be used on any size of raised bed—even ones that have already been built, if you want to jazz them up a little.

Scott McKinnon, the project's designer and builder, is always on the lookout for old pallets, fence boards, and barn boards. He's been known to make special trips to a location if he hears that something good is up for grabs. "Anything with a patina," he says. A visit to McKinnon's workshop reveals his talent for upcycling old wood that's made its way onto the back of his pickup truck and into new projects for the home.

Once you've got a selection of different types of wood, you can get started laying everything out. It takes a bit of patience and work to piece everything together for the cool effect shown here, but this "puzzle" is ultimately worth it.

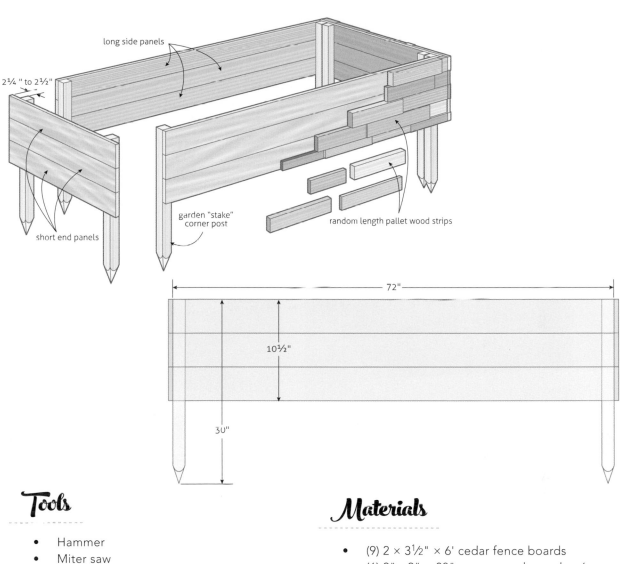

long side panels

2¼ " to 2½"

short end panels

garden "stake"
corner post

random length pallet wood strips

72"

10½"

30"

Tools

- Hammer
- Miter saw
- Cordless circular saw or a dozuki handsaw (we used a Silky woodboy—see What's a Dozuki Saw?, page 105)
- Eye and ear protection
- Work gloves

Materials

- (9) 2 × 3½" × 6' cedar fence boards
- (6) 2" ×2" × 30" spruce garden stakes (or create your own)
- Old strips of pallet wood (enough to cover the planter, approximately 30 sq. ft.)
- 1¼" finishing nails (if you're not using a pneumatic nailer)
- 1½" brass screws

Cut list

PART	DIMENSION	PCS
End panels	3½" × 3' (height × length)	6
Long panels	3½" × 6' (height × length)	6

HOW TO MAKE A
RAISED BED
WITH UPCYCLED WOOD

STEP 1: PREPARE THE LONG PANELS.

Cut three cedar fence boards in half, leaving six pieces 3 feet long. (These will be used to make the end panels. Set them aside for now.) To create the long panels, lay three 6 foot boards parallel and pushed together. Lifting the ends of the three boards together, slide a stake under the edges flush with the board ends and the flat end flush at the top. Attach with two screws per board. Attach another stake to support the center of the panel. Create the other panel in the same way with the last three 6-foot boards and stakes.

STEP 2: CUT OUT DIFFERENT LENGTHS AND TYPES OF WOOD.

Use a dozuki saw or a cordless circular saw to make quick trims here and there so you can work out the whole puzzle. Try not to place the seams close to each other. This will create a more randomized pattern. Be sure to leave some overhang at the ends, which will cover the short panels when you're putting together the whole raised bed.

STEP 3: FIGURE OUT YOUR PATTERN.
From your selection of old wood—pallet strips, old barn board, and so on—start to lay out a random pattern to cover one of these long panels. Choose different thicknesses and wood hues.

STEP 4: SECURE THE PUZZLE PIECES.
Use small finishing nails or a pneumatic nailer to attach the boards to the panels.

6

STEP 5: MAKE THE END PANELS.
Lay out three of the 3-foot boards. Place the stakes underneath as you did for the long panels, but for these, do not place them flush at the ends. Measure in 2¼ to 2½ inches, and nail the edge of the stakes. This means in each corner you'll have the two stakes meeting when the bed comes together. Repeat for the other side panel. You can now lay out a puzzle on these pieces as well.

With the stakes pointing up, assemble the four panels together and fasten with the screws. Trim the edges that you have left so that the corners are flush.

STEP 6: PLACE THE CONTAINER
IN ITS NEW HOME.
Move the raised bed to the desired location; use a large mallet or sledgehammer to drive the stakes into the ground.

7

STEP 7: LEVEL AND
SQUARE AS REQUIRED.
Use the stakes to lift the bed's corners up and down to eventually square the entire bed. Fill in the spaces with soil. Lay mulch around the outside of the bed to finish off the area.

You're now ready to fill the bed with soil and plant!

WHAT'S A DOZUKI SAW?

Dozuki saws, which originate in Japan, are handsaws with teeth that allow you to saw through wood on the pull stroke as opposed to the traditional push stroke of the more common handsaws available in North America. This useful addition to a woodworker's toolbox provides more precision when cutting softer woods. Dozuki saws can be used to cut fine joinery, like dovetails and tenons.

The dozuki saw came in handy for this project because it allows the thin pallet strips to be quickly and easily trimmed to size. A Japanese handsaw was also used to trim pieces in the cold frame project on page 208.

RAISED BED WITH BENCHES

Designed by Chris Hill for Bonnie Plants
Photography by Donna Griffith
Illustration by Len Churchill, based on Bonnie Plants plans

One of the many benefits of gardening in a raised bed is the height. Raised beds bring the garden up to you, so green thumbs who have trouble bending or squatting don't have to do so quite as much. This project takes that notion a step further by adding a special feature: benches. These are perfect for resting on while you weed. You can also use them as a place to rest your tools or a weeding bucket, a watering can, or a cup of tea—whatever you're lugging around with you as you garden. Add one bench or all four—it's entirely up to you and what you think you'll benefit from when you're puttering about in the garden. For this bed, only two benches were added, and they're both perpendicular to each other. The original plan places one bench on each opposing corner.

This garden may look complicated to build because it's so impressive-looking, but the steps are quite simple and streamlined—especially if you have your materials precut at a home improvement store.

Raised beds are also useful when the ground beneath them is compact, making it almost impossible to dig a regular garden into the ground. In this case, the raised bed is covering a mess of roots from an old bush (that had previously been removed) that were hard to dig up from the compacted earth. Before soil was added, hardware cloth was laid across the bottom, followed by a layer of landscape fabric. As a result of the depth, triple mix from a reputable soil company was used to fill a great deal of the bed, with a layer of compost dug into the top. Because of the height of this bed, make sure the area beneath will drain well as the soil dries out.

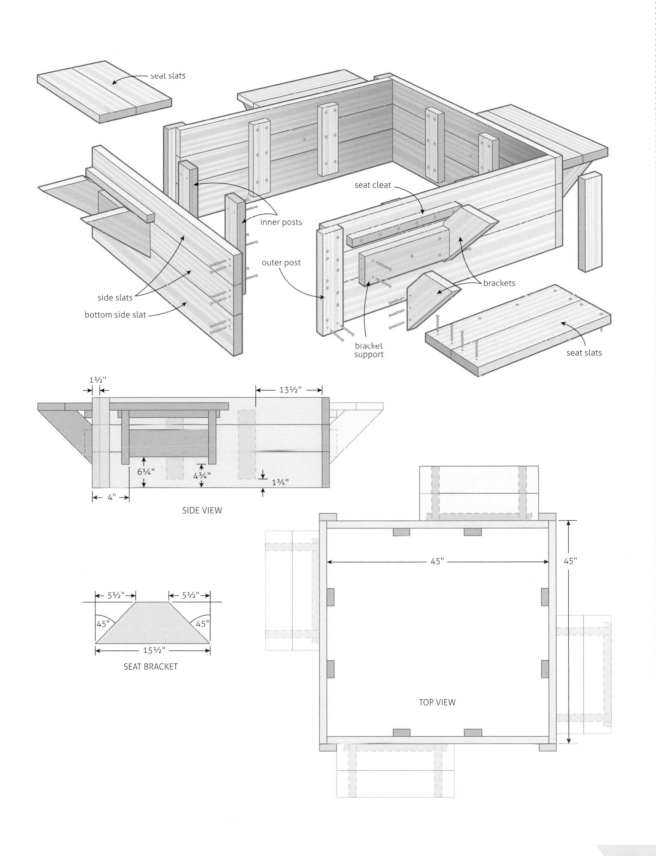

seat slats

inner posts

outer post

side slats

bottom side slat

seat cleat

brackets

bracket support

seat slats

1½"

13½"

6¾"

4¾"

1¾"

4"

SIDE VIEW

5½"

5½"

45°

45°

15½"

SEAT BRACKET

45"

45"

TOP VIEW

Tools

- Miter saw or circular saw
- Drill/driver
- Clamps
- Carpenter's square
- Tape measure
- Eye and ear protection
- Work gloves

Materials

- (1) 2 × 2" × 8' board
- (3) 2 × 4" × 8' boards
- (8) 2 × 6" × 8' boards
- (2) 2" × 8" × 8' boards
- (3) 1-lb. boxes $2\frac{1}{2}$" deck screws
- (1) 1-lb. box 3" deck screws

Cut list

PART	DIMENSION	PCS
Side slats	$1\frac{1}{2}$ × $5\frac{1}{2}$ × 45"	8
Bottom side slats	$1\frac{1}{2}$ × $7\frac{1}{4}$ × 45"	4
Inner posts	$1\frac{1}{2}$ × $3\frac{1}{2}$ × 14"	8
Bracket supports	$1\frac{1}{2}$ × $5\frac{1}{2}$ × 16"	4
Brackets	$1\frac{1}{2}$ × $5\frac{1}{2}$ × $15\frac{1}{2}$"	8
Outer posts	$1\frac{1}{2}$ × $3\frac{1}{2}$ × $16\frac{1}{2}$"	4
Seat slats	$1\frac{1}{2}$ × $5\frac{1}{2}$ × 24"	8
Seat cleats	$1\frac{1}{2}$ × $1\frac{1}{2}$ × $20\frac{1}{2}$"	4

HOW TO MAKE A
RAISED BED WITH BENCHES

1

2

STEP 1: MAKE THE SIDE ASSEMBLIES.
Create each side assembly by positioning two side slats and a bottom side slat with the ends flush. Attach the inner posts 13½ inches from the ends and 1¾ inches from the edge of the bottom side slat. Use 2½-inch deck screws to fasten. Repeat to create three more assemblies, using two side slats, one bottom side slat, and two inner posts for each. Divide the four assemblies into two sets of two.

STEP 2: ADD THE BRACKET SUPPORTS FOR THE BENCH.
Attach a bracket support to the opposite side of each assembly, overlapping the two side slats that will be closest to the top. Fasten in place with 2½-inch deck screws.

STEP 3: CONNECT THE BRACKETS.
Attach the brackets to both the bracket support and the side slats with 2½-inch deck screws.

STEP 4: JOIN THE SEAT CLEAT.
Place the seat cleat flush with the brackets, and attach it to the side slats with 2½-inch deck screws.

STEP 5: ADD THE SEAT SLATS.
Set the first seat slat in place and attach it to both the cleat and the brackets with 2½-inch deck screws.

STEP 6: ATTACH THE SECOND SEAT SLAT.
Using a ¼-inch scrap piece of wood as a spacer, set the second seat slat in place and attach it to the brackets. Then remove the spacer.

STEP 7: JOIN THE OUTER POSTS.
Attach an outer post to the sides of two of the side assemblies. It should be placed on the outside with half covering the wood and half overlapping.

STEP 8: JOIN TOGETHER
THE FIRST SET OF SIDE ASSEMBLIES.
Attach one assembly with the outer post to another, making sure the ends of the side assemblies sit flush with the outer posts. Fasten with 3-inch deck screws. Place in the garden where you want the raised bed to go.

9

STEP 9: FIT ALL THE SIDES TOGETHER.
Attach the remaining side assemblies with 3-inch deck screws. They should fit together snugly, like a puzzle.

PLANT IT!

Having more than one raised bed makes it easy to separate vegetables that don't do well together and pairing them with ones that do. This is called "companion planting." In this case, members of the Brassica family—kohlrabi and cauliflower—were planted with onions, beets, cucumber, and squash. However, tomatoes, for example, do not thrive with Brassicas, so they were planted in another bed.

If you have only one raised bed, you can separate edible foes by planting them a few rows over.

UTILITY RAISED BED

If aesthetics are not an issue, then this no-frills, functional raised bed may be just what you need to grow a high volume of produce. This bed is considerably longer than any of the other projects in this section, but it's 5 feet wide. This should still make it accessible to weed and plant by reaching in from the outside. Big beds like this one are great for crops where you want to plant a lot of one variety, like corn or pickling cucumbers. This project also provides a lesson in how to reinforce the sides. Many raised beds are made from stacked boards secured in the corners, but on the long ends they can curve inward or outward over time. Tie rods have been used here to provide plenty of support and keep beds square.

Tools

- Circular saw or sliding miter saw
- Drill
- Countersink bit
- $\frac{1}{2}$" spade bit
- Wrench
- Shovel
- Eye and ear protection
- Work gloves

Materials

- (8) 2 × 6" ×16' cedar
- (1) 2 × 6" × 8' (for braces)
- (4) $\frac{1}{2}$" × 6' galvanized tie rods with washers and bolts
- (5 lbs.) $2\frac{1}{2}$" deck screws

Cut list

PART	DIMENSION	PCS
Side	$1\frac{1}{2} \times 5\frac{1}{2}$" × 16'	6
End	$1\frac{1}{2} \times 5\frac{1}{2}$" × 5'	6
Braces	$1\frac{1}{2} \times 5\frac{1}{2}$" × 15'	12

HOW TO MAKE THE
UTILITY RAISED BED

STEP 1: BUILD THE FRAME.

Start by screwing together the first level (sides to ends), predrilling the holes with a countersink bit so you don't split the ends. After the first level is done, attach vertical 2 × 6 braces at the inside corners. Add the next layer of sides and ends, alternating the lengths to make the corners a little tighter and more interesting-looking. The sides and ends are all equal lengths, so adjoining corners are alternated in opposite ways, and the overall size of the raised bed is 5 × 16 feet. Attach more vertical 2 × 6 braces every 4 or 5 feet on the inside of the boards.

2

STEP 2: BRACE THE FRAME.

A long raised bed built from 2 × 6s needs to be held together at the center or it will bow out from the weight of the dirt. Add a 2 × 6 vertical support and drill two ½-inch-diameter holes at the same points on both sides.

Push galvanized, threaded tie rods through the holes, and then thread galvanized washers and nuts over the ends. Tighten until the distance at the center and the ends is the same. Threaded tie rods are zinc-plated, usually ⅜, ½, or ⅝ inch in diameter, that are tapped with threads over the entire length. If gaps eventually appear at the corners, dig out some of the adjoining soil to reduce the pressure, push the walls back together as best you can, and reinforce the corners with large metal angles. Trim off any protruding hardware.

TIP:
A center divider could also be created out of wood.

RAISED BED WITH A POND

Designed and photographed by Melissa J. Will

Melissa J. Will, who runs the fantastic, idea-packed DIY blog *Empress of Dirt*, created the pond in a raised bed that you see pictured here. It turned out that the spot where she wanted to place a pond couldn't be dug out because of underground cables, so she adapted her original plan and built up instead of down.

One of the benefits of putting a pond in a raised bed, says Will, is the accessibility it provides. Raising it up makes it much easier to access the pond filter pump for maintenance than if the pond were in the ground.

The first step of this project is to make a raised bed, which you can create using any of the plans provided in this book, adapted to the length, width, and height requirements that will be determined by the pond form or liner that you choose.

ABOVE: Embellishments add to a pond's whimsy and visual interest as a garden.

OPPOSITE: Raised beds can be useful for more than simply planting edibles. They can hold an entire water garden!

HOW TO MAKE A
RAISED BED WITH A POND

Materials

- Raised bed built to fit the pond liner
- Pond form or liner that fits the length, width, and height of your raised bed (however, even if it doesn't, you can fill the surrounding area with soil and plant around it)
- Flat-bottomed rocks or stepping stones to hold the liner lip down
- Recirculating pond pump made for the size of the pond—a 450-gallon pond needs a 450 gph pump
- Soil to fill in the space between the pond form and the bed
- Access to a ground-fault circuit interrupter (GFCI) outdoor electrical outlet for running the pump

STEP 1: INSERT THE POND FORM IN THE RAISED BED.
Gently fill in the spaces around the pond form with soil, making sure it all fits together snugly.

STEP 2: FIND A PLACE FOR POND ACCESSORIES.
Figure out how you want to arrange the circulating pump and where the electrical cord will go. You may want to conceal it on the side that gets the least amount of foot traffic. Follow the instructions that come with the kit to set everything up safely. If you're not comfortable dealing with the electrical components, hire an electrician to set it up for you.

STEP 3: FILL THE POND WITH WATER.
Wait for two to three days before adding your water plants, recommends Will. This allows the chlorine in the water to offgas. She also says to wait a couple of weeks before adding fish—they won't like the chlorine either.

PLANT IT!

Will recommends looking for hardy perennial aquatic plants rather than annuals, which only last for one season. Add decorative features to the side as she has done here.

SIX EDIBLE,
WATER-LOVING PLANTS

Fern Ridge Landscaping is a landscape design company that focuses on eco-consulting and creating environmentally sustainable gardens. Owner Sean James is an encyclopedia of knowledge when it comes to plants, especially native species.

If you're interested in exploring growing edible water plants, James recommends the following varieties. However, it should be noted that any water plants that you consume should be boiled first to eliminate any harmful organisms.

Marsh marigold

Pickerel weed

Arrowhead

Watercress

Cattail

Photos: *Sean James*

Water hyacinth

OTHER WAYS TO BUILD RAISED BEDS

When it comes to raised bed design, there are so many avenues you can take. Some might be trickier than others to execute, so if you're building a raised bed yourself, opt for a simpler design for your first one. That way you can get planting sooner!

You can be as creative as you like, or simply opt for a utilitarian look that gets the job done. The end result—fresh, homegrown produce—will be the same no matter what your raised bed happens to look like. Here are a few other easy and more complicated construction ideas.

WHEN LIFE GIVES YOU LEMONS, BUILD A RAISED BED

A multitude of tree trunks felled by an incredibly destructive pest. What do you do? "For those who are looking to save a buck or who are more into a freestyle design, an inexpensive way to create a raised bed is to use waste wood in place of timbers," says landscape designer Sean James, whose company, Fern Ridge Landscaping, put these beds together. "These ash logs were taken down as a result of the invasive emerald ash borer, but they've found new life as a garden," he says. In this case, there was no construction work necessary. Logs were simply laid in a raised bed shape and the area was filled accordingly with soil.

ABOVE: "Having logs slowly breaking down is excellent for biodiversity!" says James, who advises that you never move wood beyond a quarantine zone if it has been infected by an invasive pest. *Sean James*

LEFT: Finials, paint, and levels make for a visually interesting raised bed.

STACK TIMBERS INTO A RAISED BED

Perhaps the easiest way to build a raised bed that doesn't really require much woodworking know-how is to stack timbers and stagger the end joints—like you'd see with a log cabin. To fasten everything together, hammer landscape spikes into all four corners and, voilà, a raised bed.

PILING ROCKS AND BRICKS

If you have a pile of old interlocking brick or rocks that don't yet have a purpose in your garden, stack them to create a raised bed. If possible, try to stagger each piece to add more stability to your structure.

ABOVE: If you don't happen to have a neglected pile, check out a site such as Craigslist to see if someone in your area happens to be giving materials away. *Sean James*

TOP LEFT: The most basic raised bed is simply made from landscape timbers with staggered end joints. This one is lined with landscape fabric.

MIDDLE LEFT: This brand new raised bed was built from timbers. *Bren Haas*

LEFT: Though timber raised beds look polished and new when they're first built, over time they will age to a nice faded patina. *Bren Haas*

WEAVE A RAISED BED FROM WATTLE

Wattle is a term used to describe a technique for weaving a fence or structure from twigs and sticks around stakes. You need to use young wood that will bend easily as you weave it in and out of the stakes. Weed trees are great for this because you don't need to worry about sacrificing a good tree in the name of garden art. This technique used to be popular for building fences that would contain livestock, but nowadays it's more of a decorative feature. Think of the side of a basket.

Wattling is also a great technique for building decorative plant supports.

ENCLOSE A RAISED BED WITH CONCRETE BLOCKS

Concrete blocks are like ready-made walls for your raised bed. There's no woodworking or assembly involved; you simply outline the area where you'd like a raised bed, make sure it's level, and then line 'em up! You even get a bonus growing area—fill the block holes with the same healthy soil you used to fill your bed, and fill those with plants too. If you want the border to be more decorative, fill the holes with drought-tolerant sedum or other low-maintenance plants.

TOP: Wattle makes for a gorgeous, rustic-looking raised bed.

MIDDLE: Protect the sides of the bed with plastic to avoid rot. Cable ties can be used to fasten the sides together. *Niki Jabbour*

BOTTOM: Be careful not to use cinder blocks, which look the same as concrete blocks, especially if you're growing food, because they may contain fly ash, a harmful contaminant. *Amy Andrychowicz*

BUILD A STRAW BALE BED

A straw bale garden, a concept made popular by author and gardener Joel Karsten, is another type of raised bed. Straw bales can be used to outline a temporary raised bed, or you can actually use them as a raised bed by planting right into the bale itself. Just be sure to use straw rather than hay because hay can contain unwanted seeds that will root in your garden.

MAKE A RAISED BED WITH HALF-LAP JOINTS

For experienced woodworkers, making a half-lap joint is a great technique that can be applied to a raised bed design. Basically, you're stacking T- and upside-down-T-shaped wood with half of the corners cut out. Not only does this make the bed stronger, it also makes for a visually interesting raised bed. (Half-lap joints were also used to strengthen the structure that became the greenhouse on page 216.)

Any square-edged timber can be used to make a half-lap joint—4 × 4, 4 × 6, 6 × 6, and so on—which is essentially notching out exactly half of the thickness (or depth) for each piece that will be matched together. A thickness planer can be used to ensure each piece of wood has the exact same dimensions before you get started.

ABOVE: Straw bales make for instant raised beds— no construction required.

BOTTOM LEFT AND RIGHT: Half-lap joints can be created out of cut boards or rounded timber. This construction makes for a neat, aesthetically pleasing design.

CUTTING HALF-LAP JOINTS

Lay out and stack your wood so that the most flattering sides will be facing outward. Mark whether the pieces will be cut from the top or the bottom.

Choose your pieces of wood, and place the flattest side of each one face-down on a work surface. Mark the wood 3½ inches from the end, and use a ruler to draw a straight line. Set the cutting depth of your circular saw to 1¾ inches, and cut along the 3½-inch end. Repeat this step until you have a series of parallel cuts that are about ¼ inch apart (photo A). These are called "kerf cuts." Use a hammer or a mallet to chip away at the cut pieces (photo B). Clean up the area with a wood chisel because you want the boards to rest flat when you stack them.

Once all of your half-lap joints have been cut, test-fit all the corners by restacking the raised bed and then attach.

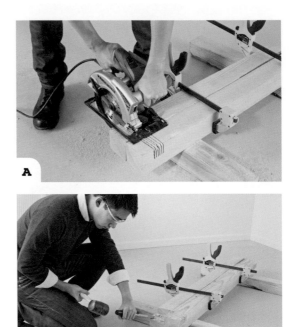

A

B

BELOW: Weld a raised bed out of metal: If you'd like to hire a professional welder, steel makes for a durable raised bed. It also develops a lovely rust-colored patina over time. *Orchard People*

PLANTING GARLIC
IN RAISED BEDS

Raised beds provide an optimum area for growing garlic. The soil is friable and not compacted because you've added and amended it yourself, and the bed likely drains well, so the cloves you plant should not rot as they're trying to grow. A nice loose soil also helps to produce bigger bulbs because nothing is obstructing their growth.

Some nurseries carry garlic, but you can also purchase it online. It's usually available starting in late summer so that you can plant it in the fall, anywhere from three to five weeks before the ground freezes. Softneck garlic varieties thrive in warmer climates. As the growing zones get cooler, hardneck garlic becomes a hardier option that is more commonly grown in northern gardens.

When you're getting ready to plant, be sure to amend the soil with some composted manure to add some nutrients back in if you've just pulled out all your summer crops.

Also, if you have more than one raised bed, remember that the space you choose to plant the garlic will be occupied until about late July or early August, when garlic is generally ready to harvest. Choose your sunniest spot. If you only have one raised bed, choose a smaller section for the garlic so that you have room for other crops come spring.

Keep in mind that garlic doesn't like to be planted near peas and beans (both the pole and bush variety) and vice versa, so be sure there is space between them if you're planting in the same bed.

When figuring out how much to purchase and grow, remember that you plant single cloves that you carefully separate from a head. One head of garlic can yield anywhere from four to eight cloves. Plant the biggest ones in the garden. To plant, place the clove pointy side up in the soil about 2 to 3 inches deep, and leave about 6 to 8 inches between each clove in all directions. Give the raised bed a good watering. Add a layer of straw mulch (not hay because it contains seeds) to keep everything nice and cozy over the winter. This will also help keep the weeds to a minimum—you don't want anything competing below the soil with the garlic bulbs.

TOP: Rick Weingarden, co-owner of Anything Grows Seed Company, uses his raised bed to grow the following garlic varieties: Music, Red Russian, German Red, and Siberian. He says he only plants the large cloves (and eats the small ones), which over the years has resulted in bigger bulbs. *Rick Weingarden*

RIGHT: I like to plant different varieties of garlic each year in my raised beds to see if I can discern between the various flavor profiles. My favorite garlic variety is French Rocambole. *Tara Nolan*

ABOVE: Channel your inner bricklayer: Bricks are used to make the raised beds shown in this photo from intrepid traveler Donna Dawson of www.gardeningtours.com. These raised beds are part of the sunken vegetable gardens at Beechwood Gardens in Johannesburg, South Africa. *Donna Dawson*

ABOVE RIGHT: Raised beds in the buff: This raised bed shows that simply raising the soil higher than the ground surrounding it could technically be considered a raised bed. It just takes a bit more effort to keep it neat and tidy. *Niki Jabbour*

MIDDLE: The closer: While it may not provide a ton of support over time, a simple metal bracket fastened around each corner of four boards that are set up to become a raised bed can still create very functional garden. *Jessica Walliser*

RIGHT: Robust raised bed materials: The slabs of concrete used to build these sturdy- and stocky-looking raised beds ensure that nothing will be going anywhere for some time. *Jessica Walliser*

SUCCESSION PLANTING IN RAISED BEDS

With raised beds, you don't have to limit your growing period to one season. You can plant cool-weather crops, like peas and broccoli, in the spring, heat-seekers, like tomatoes and peppers, for a summer harvest, and so on. When one crop comes out, another can be waiting in the wings (or under your grow lights), ready to be dug in. It takes a little bit of planning, but succession planting is the key to a continuous, fruitful harvest from early spring right up until the snow flies.

One way to keep track of everything is to keep a list of early-, mid-, and late-season crops that you want to plant so that you know what is maturing when.

Many only consider using their grow lights in the winter to produce spring seedlings. However, a grow light system is a great tool for more advanced green thumbs who want to keep producing high-quality seedlings for summer and autumn succession planting.

You can also stagger succession planting. For example, if you're sowing lettuce seeds, rather than planting them all at once, sow them a few days apart so that as you're harvesting one row, another is filling in. You can do this with lots of different crops, from root veggies to climbing edibles, such as peas and beans.

ABOVE: Grow lights can help you get a head start on crops. *Niki Jabbour*

LEFT: Once the lettuce started to bolt in these raised beds, it was removed to make way for a new crop. *Paul Zammit*

THE PERFECT LEVEL:
A RAISED BED THAT MAKES GARDENING POSSIBLE

One of the benefits of gardening in raised beds that's emphasized throughout this book is that they can be customized to suit a variety of requirements. A simple matter of height can be a big deal to an eager green thumb—and the difference between gardening and not gardening. Here, gardener Verna Kakowchyk explains how her raised beds allowed her to discover the satisfaction of growing her own edibles:

My husband, Rod, built these raised gardens for me approximately eight years ago. I had always said I did not want a garden that I had to bend over in order to work in it. And, unless I had a raised garden that was waist high where I could reach across it while working in the garden, I wasn't interested in gardening. "Be careful what you wish for" is very true because while I was recovering from a serious car accident, Rod built the raised gardens you see here.

All the wood used to make these raised beds is reclaimed. Most of it came from an old deck that we had removed from the front of the house. We salvaged as much of the wood as possible and used it for the sides and ends, as well as for the support board under the bins.

TOP: Kakowchyk likes to plant a variety of edibles, herbs, and lettuces. Dwarf varieties of certain veggies, such as beans, provide more space for other plants.

BOTTOM: Dill, Italian basil, Swiss chard, and carrots are planted in bins that are suspended from the raised bed frame.

Images courtesy of Verna Kakowchyk

There are five large black bins that sit in each of the two raised gardens. They were sourced from a plastics company that was intending to recycle them. Drainage holes were drilled in the bottom of each bin, which were then lined with landscape fabric and filled with gardening soil.

Since the bins are heavy under the weight of the soil, the wide board running underneath the full length of the raised garden gives extra support to the bins. It is 2 × 10 inches wide. That support beam is attached to the edges and acts as a brace for the bins that are held in place by hanging inside the framework of the garden. The legs supporting the front and back of the raised gardens are reclaimed fence posts.

The cement pad on which the raised garden is located started out as a kennel for our three Dobermans. Afterward, it became a miniature version of a basketball court with a hoop, and then finally it was the perfect location for our raised gardens.

The top edges of the bins are at about waist height, making it easy for me to access the garden. I grow a variety of items each year, including dwarf beans, chives, sweet basil, cilantro, a variety of mixed lettuce, dill, Italian basil, 'Bright Lights' Swiss chard, carrots, radishes, and thyme.

TOP: The width of this raised bed was customized so that the black plastic bins could comfortably hang along the top edge.

MIDDLE: A long board is attached to the underside of the raised bed frame and acts as a support beam.

BOTTOM: A view of both of Verna's raised beds.

Images courtesy of Verna Kakowchyk

CHAPTER 4

RAISED BEDS FOR SMALL SPACES

Who says you can't have a vegetable garden if you happen to have a tiny space? Be it a balcony, a rooftop patio, or a small urban yard, if you're lucky enough to have sunlight, your green thumb just needs to get a little creative. Of course there are unique challenges, such as strong wind gusts if you're high up. But a few tricks here and there will help to customize your space according to the conditions presented by the chosen space for your garden. And this doesn't just mean a few herbs and a couple of tomatoes. You can grow root vegetables and cucumbers and even melons in a small area.

Just a few square feet can support a raised bed that will provide a bounty of fresh produce. The increasing popularity of vertical gardening means there are also lots of kits available to consumers now that will help support dreams of a harvest, even high up.

The ideas in this section include getting creative with vintage finds and giving them a modern spin, discovering ready-made kits and applying a tiered approach to the typical idea of what a raised bed is.

As for what you can grow? Well, pretty much anything—within reason. When it comes to tomatoes, for example, opt for bushy, dwarf varieties that are more compact. Choose mini versions of pumpkins instead of the ones that will win medals for their girth at fall fairs. And for vining plants like cucumbers, think about growing up rather than out. If not enough sun is an issue, you may not be able to grow the heat-seekers like peppers, but you just might have a thriving mini plot full of beans and greens, including lettuce and spinach.

As with a large space, trial and error will help you determine what will grow best in the small space that you have.

This church has made great use of a flat expanse of roof. Several raised beds bursting with produce have been placed in a spot that clearly offers prime growing conditions. *Jenny Rhodenizer*

Modular raised bed projects allow you to tailor the size and shape to your space. The raised bed shown here uses square boxes surrounded by concrete blocks.

At the Fairmont Royal York in Toronto, 17 four-poster raised beds cover the roof along with multiple pots and a buzzing apiary that produces award-winning honey. *Fairmont Hotels & Resorts*

Many Fairmont Hotels & Resorts properties feature herbicide- and pesticide-free kitchen gardens where their chefs can pick fresh produce for their fine dining restaurants. And for some of these properties, rooftops provide that optimum growing space. Fairmont The Queen Elizabeth's garden in Montreal has been on the 22nd floor since 2011. It uses a low-maintenance, self-sufficient drip system to water and fertilize plants. *Fairmont Hotels & Resorts*

Forgotten corners of the yard provide great spots to grow edibles. Just be certain that they receive six to eight hours of sunlight a day. Or grow vegetables that are shade tolerant, such as spinach. *Tara Nolan*

Get creative with empty crates that used to hold products such as wine bottles or apples. Use landscape fabric to fill any gaps where soil could escape, and be sure to use a good-quality potting soil so that plants can thrive. *Tara Nolan*

Fabric gardens not only come in handy shapes with sturdy bases that you can set anywhere, they also come in hanging varieties that allow you to use valuable wall or balcony railing space to grow small edibles.
© Les Urbainculteurs/Smart Pots

You can also use fabric gardens to grow hardy ornamental plants, such as this sedum. *Tara Nolan*

Giant wooden wine crates are deep enough to grow fruit trees. *Niki Jabbour*

An empty, accessible rooftop may provide the perfect space to host a raised bed—or two or three! Just be sure to consult a structural engineer before loading up a roof with multiple beds.

Fabric pots make for lightweight gardens that can be arranged on balconies. © *Du Monde au Balcon*

Many municipalities are now requiring building designers to incorporate green roof elements into their blueprints.

Rooftops such as this one on a convention center present perfect garden locations in an urban setting. © *Les Urbainculteurs / Smart Pots*

VERTICAL HERB (OR LETTUCE) PLANTER

Designed by Chris Hill for Bonnie Plants
Photography by Donna Griffith
Illustration by Len Churchill, based on Bonnie Plants plans

What's the solution for a small, compact area where you want to grow food, but don't believe you have the space? Grow up! Vertical gardening has become popular in urban areas where outdoor expanses can be rather limited. This planter allows for a very thorough variety of herbs to be planted that you can enjoy in summer meals—basil, dill, oregano, chives, and more. Lettuce would do equally well in this vertical raised bed—you can basically grow a whole salad bar right outside your door. You just need at least six to eight hours of sunlight in your small space per day in order for your edibles to flourish.

There's even a bonus section to this planter along the top, where you can tuck in a few dramatic "spillers," such as nasturtiums—also completely edible—and "fillers," such as fragrant lemongrass. Strawberries would also do well up here because the runners can cascade over the sides.

Building this project looks daunting, but it's relatively easy. It really comes down to lots of measuring and small pieces to install. If you've gone the herb route, be sure to give your plants a regular haircut. Herbs benefit from this quick and easy maintenance task for a couple of reasons. First, it helps the plant fill out as it grows. Second, it helps prevent the herbs from flowering, so they'll last longer.

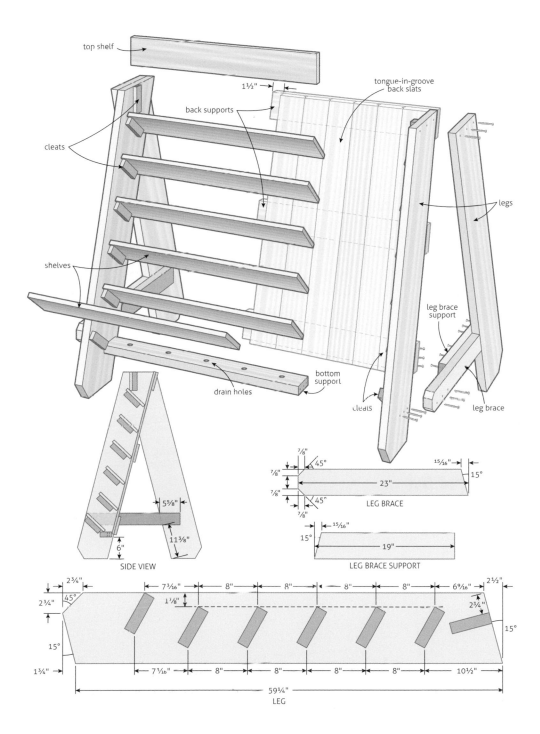

top shelf

1½"

tongue-in-groove
back slats

back supports

cleats

legs

shelves

leg brace
support

bottom
support

drain holes

cleats

leg brace

SIDE VIEW

5⅝"

11⅜"

6"

⅞"
⅞"
⅞"
45°
⅞"
45°

23"

15°

15/16"

LEG BRACE

15°

15/16"

19"

LEG BRACE SUPPORT

2¾"
45°
2¾"
1⅞"
15°
1¾"

7³/₁₆"
8"
8"
8"
8"
6⁹/₁₆"
2½"

2¾"
15°

7¹/₁₆"
8"
8"
8"
8"
10½"

59¼"

LEG

Tools

- Miter saw or circular saw
- Drill/driver
- Clamps
- Carpenter's square
- Tape measure
- Eye and ear protection
- Work gloves

Materials

- (1) 1 × 2" × 8' board
- (1) 1 × 4" × 8' board
- (2) 1 × 6" × 8' boards
- (6) 1 × 6" × 8' tongue-and-groove boards
- (2) 1 × 8" × 8' boards
- (1) 2 × 4" × 8' board
- (2) 2 × 10" × 10' boards
- (68) 1¼" deck screws
- (18) 2½" deck screws
- Sealer (optional)

Cut list

PART	DIMENSION	PCS
Legs	1½ × 9¼ × 59¼"	4
Leg braces (see illustration for special cuts)	1½ × 3½ × 23"	2
Leg brace supports (see illustration for special cuts)	¾ × 3½ × 19"	2
Cleats	¾ × 1½ × 5½"	14
Back slats	⅝ × 5½ × 50"	6
Back supports	¾ × 5½ × 33½"	3
Bottom support	1 ½ × 3½ × 30½"	1
Top shelf	¾ × 5½ × 30½"	1
Shelves	¾ × 7¼ × 30½"	6

HOW TO MAKE A
VERTICAL HERB PLANTER

STEP 1: PREPARE THE LEG ASSEMBLIES.
Attach the cleats to the inside of the legs. These will be used to support the shelves.

STEP 2: CREATE THE FRAME.
The end assemblies are braced A-frames made from natural cedar. Make the leg assemblies by cutting the 2 × 10s, lining up the ends, and attaching with screws.

STEP 3: CREATE THE LEG SUPPORTS.
Lay out and cut the ends of the leg brace support and leg brace according to the illustration on page 139. Attach with 2½-inch screws on the inside and 1¼-inch screws on the outside.

Attach the bottom support to the leg assemblies.

STEP 4: ASSEMBLE THE BACK SLATS.
Fit the back slats together to create a solid panel. After fitting the back slats, measure the width of the panel to make sure you have the proper overhang on the back supports.

Attach the three back supports to the back slats.

STEP 5: FASTEN THE BACK SLATS TO THE LEGS.
Set the back assembly in place between the leg assemblies and flush against the bottom support, and attach.

STEP 6: ADD DRAINAGE HOLES.
Drill drain holes in the bottom support in line with the grooves in the back slats.

STEP 7: SECURE THE TOP AND BOTTOM SHELVES.
Attach the top shelf to the top cleats using 1¼-inch screws.

8

STEP 8: SLIDE IN THE SHELVES
OVER THE CLEATS.
Place the bottom shelf on the bottom cleats, and
start adding the first layer of soil. Insert the next
shelf on the cleats and add the next layer of soil.
Continue adding shelves and soil to the rest of
the planter. Adjust the shelves to allow the soil
to cascade down to the level below. Manipulate
the soil on each level as you plant. You'll need
to make several adjustments during this process.
Make sure the soil continues to cascade down
until it's set in place. Place two to three plants on
each level for the best results. Water the base of
the plants thoroughly, making sure to limit the
amount of water that falls directly onto the leaves
of the plants. Applying a sealer to the bottom of
the leg braces will help to limit moisture-wicking.

HOW TO PRESERVE YOUR HERBS

Herbs benefit from a regular haircut. It helps the plant
fill out and become bushier as it grows and it prevents
herbs from flowering.

When you give your herbs their regular trim, you
may not be able to use them in your cooking right away.
But there are a few ways to preserve herbs. One is to tie

them with twine and allow them to hang upside down
in a well-ventilated space. To keep the dust away, tie a
paper bag with several cuts in it around the bunches.

Another way to preserve herbs? Freeze them. Herbs
that freeze well include chives, basil, parsley, and rosemary.

ELEVATED PLANTER BOX

Designed by (and kit and step-by-steps
provided by) Freedom Growing
Photography by Donna Griffith

With the rising popularity of raised beds, companies are coming up with easy-to-assemble kits that don't require many tools or a ton of woodworking expertise. Materials generally come pre-cut with detailed step-by-step instructions, depending on the project. This one, designed by a company called Freedom Growing, uses galvanized, powder-coated steel to create a sturdy base into which cedar boards are placed and then attached by stainless-steel bolts.

This Elevated Planter Box model comes in a variety of eye-catching colors that make it a conversation piece before you've even added the plants.

While having a kit mailed to your home is convenient, be sure to look into what the shipping charges will be. A quick online search will reveal companies that may be creating raised bed kits in your area, meaning you can arrange for a local delivery or even pick it up yourself. Local nurseries or home-improvement stores may offer ready-to-make kits as well.

Tools

- Phillips screwdriver
- $^7/_{16}$" ratcheting socket wrench
- Eye protection
- Work gloves

Materials

(All the following are included with the kit)

- 4 long rails
- 4 legs
- 4 short rails
- (32) $^1/_2$" carriage bolts
- (32) 1" carriage bolts
- (32) lock washers
- (32) flat washers
- (64) nuts
- (2) long cedar boards
- (2) long cedar boards with rounded edge
- (2) short cedar boards
- (2) short cedar boards with rounded edge
- (6) slats
- (1) 2 × 4" center support beam
- (1) piece of lining material

HOW TO MAKE AN
ELEVATED PLANTER BOX

METAL FRAME ASSEMBLY

STEP 1: UNPACK AND START WITH THE LEG ASSEMBLIES.

Unpack all parts onto a soft surface to prevent marking of powder-coated finish on the product. For this project, landscape fabric was used to keep all the pieces safe. All steps are to be hand-tightened until all the parts are in place.

Lay one long rail on a soft surface with the channel facing up. Lay two of the legs flat on the ground on either side of the long rail. Slide the bottom of the leg underneath the long rail, matching up the hole patterns on each end of the long rail. (To tell the difference between the top and bottom of the leg, the $\frac{1}{2}$-inch bends in the leg are close to the bottom.)

Attach the long rail to the inside of the bottom of the leg with a $\frac{1}{2}$-inch carriage bolt, through the holes of the legs and long rails. Secure the bolt with a lock washer and nut per hole. Make sure the nut and washer sit inside the channel with the bolt head on the outside of the leg. Hand-tighten.

STEP 2: ADD THE REMAINING RAILS.

Lay another long rail on the same legs just above the $\frac{1}{2}$-inch bend of the leg, matching up the hole patterns. Attach the long rail to the inside of the legs by inserting a $\frac{1}{2}$-inch carriage bolt, through the holes of both the leg and long rail. Secure the bolt with a one-lock washer and one nut per hole. Make sure the nut and washer sit inside the channel with the bolt head on the outside of the leg. Hand-tighten, and set aside the assembly.

Repeat the previous steps using the remaining legs and long rails.

2

3

STEP 3: FASTEN THE SHORT RAILS.

While one of the assemblies from above is still laying down, match the hole pattern on the bottom of the leg with a short rail, so the short rail is standing straight up in the air with the channel facing inward. Attach the short rails to the inside of the leg by inserting a ½-inch carriage bolt through the predrilled holes and securing the bolt with one lock washer and one nut per each hole; there are two holes. Make sure the nut and washer sit inside the channel with the bolt head on the outside of the leg. Hand-tighten until all of the rails are attached. Now repeat this process on the other leg.

Stand up another short rail on the same legs just above the ½-inch bend of the leg, matching up the hole patterns. Attach the short rails to the inside of the center of the legs by inserting a ½-inch carriage bolt through the predrilled holes and securing the bolt with one lock washer and one nut per hole; there are two holes per leg. Make sure the nut and washer sit inside the channel with the bolt head on the outside of the leg. Hand-tighten until all of the rails are attached. Repeat this process on the other leg.

STEP 4: ADD THE FINISHING TOUCHES TO THE FRAME.

To complete the metal frame, match up the hole patterns of both halves of the legs and rails, and attach the pieces together by inserting ½-inch carriage bolts through the predrilled holes and securing the bolts with one lock washer and one nut per hole. Make sure the nut and washer sit inside the channel with the bolt head on the outside of the leg. Once all of the bolts and nuts are in place, tighten all of the nuts and bolts using the $7/16$-inch ratcheting socket wrench, making sure the bolt heads sit flush on the legs. Be careful to not over-tighten.

Place the 2 × 4 center support beam into the center of the top short rails. Do this by putting the 2 × 4 in horizontally and twisting it so the slots cut in the beam fit snuggly on the bends of the short rails.

WOOD BOX ASSEMBLY

Note: Freedom Growing recommends applying a finish or paint to the outside of the cedar before you assemble the box.

STEP 1: FIT THE BOARDS IN PLACE.

With the frame right-side up, place the long cedar boards with predrilled holes on the long sides of the frame, making sure the countersunk holes face inside the box. Match up the pre-drilled holes with the square holes in the steel frame, and attach the wood to the metal frame using the 1-inch carriage bolts, flat washer, and nut. Make sure the carriage bolt head is on the outside of the frame and the washer and nut are on the inside of the box. Repeat on the other side. Tighten all of the nuts and bolts using the 7/16-inch ratcheting socket wrench. Do not over-tighten or you may split the cedar.

(Hint: If the holes are not lining up, flip over the boards or try it on the other side. Or put the tip of a screwdriver in the holes and wiggle it around until the holes line up. Make sure the square shaft of the carriage bolt sits flush inside the square hole of the steel frame.)

Place the short cedar boards with predrilled holes on the end of the frame, making sure the countersunk holes face inside the box. Match up the predrilled holes with the square holes in the steel frame, and attach the wood to the metal frame using the 1-inch carriage bolts, flat washer, and nut. Make sure the carriage bolt head is on the outside of the frame and the washer and nut are on the inside of the box. Repeat on the other end. Tighten all of the nuts and bolts using the 7/16-inch-long ratcheting socket wrench. Do not over-tighten or you may split the cedar.

Place the long cedar boards with predrilled holes and rounded edge on the long sides of the frame, rounded side up, making sure the countersunk holes face inside the box and the rounded edge is right-side up facing the inside of the box. Match up the predrilled holes on the boards and legs, and attach the wood to the metal frame using the 1-inch carriage bolts, flat washer, and nut. Make sure the carriage bolt head is on the outside of the frame and the washer and nut are on the inside of the box. Repeat on the other side. Tighten all of the nuts and bolts using the 7/16-inch-long ratcheting socket wrench. Do not over-tighten or you may split the cedar.

Repeat these steps for the short cedar boards.

Place the slats inside the box, leaving a small gap between the boards for drainage.

STEP 2: LINE YOUR RAISED BED.
Use the landscape fabric provided with the kit to line the box. Cedar will turn a grayish-silver color over time, so Freedom Growing recommends sealing or clear-coating the outside only of the cedar with a nontoxic clear sealer such as beeswax, linseed oil, or tung oil. These are available at most hardware stores. Sealing the wood will help extend the life of the cedar.

You can also turn your planter box into a mini greenhouse or cold frame by adding a cover.

Freedom Growing recommends that kit owners check the integrity of the wood every year before planting to make sure the cedar doesn't need replacing and that the nuts and bolts are still tight.

Note: Depending on the soil type you use, a filled garden box can weigh as much as 200 pounds.

PLANT IT!

For newbie gardeners who may not know what to plant, or for green thumbs who need a little planting inspiration, Freedom Growing provides recipe cards with their kits that offer suggestions.

This box used their Salsa Garden guidelines—with a few additions and omissions. Here's what was planted:

Herbs: rosemary, parsley, cilantro
Marigolds
Nasturtiums (2)
Onions

Pepper (1)
Swiss chard
Tomatoes (2)

Bamboo mini trellises were added at the time of planting to stake the tomatoes and the peppers.

4 REASONS TO PLANT ORNAMENTALS IN YOUR RAISED BEDS

1. Ornamentals can act as natural pest control in the garden. Borage flowers, for example, are said to repel hornworms, while marigolds (a common sight in raised beds) are said to repel root-knot nematodes that can damage melons, and they keep harmful nematodes away from the brassica family.

2. Ornamental flowers can attract beneficial insects, like predatory wasps and flies, that will make short work of the bad guys that try to infiltrate your beds. Sweet alyssum will attract hover flies, whose larvae can eliminate leafhoppers that might try to destroy eggplant and tomato crops. *Niki Jabbour*

3. Ornamental blooms can attract pollinators, such as bees and butterflies, thus improving your edible yield. Plant zinnias, poppies, heirloom varieties of sunflowers, and nasturtiums. *Tara Nolan*

4. And . . . they look good! Ornamental blooms add visual interest to veggie gardens.

Not only are nasturtiums edible (both the leaves and the blooms), they're also great trap crops for aphids. And they repel various other pests, like whitofly, cucumber beetles, and squash bugs. Be sure to plant a few of these trailing beauties in your raised beds. *Niki Jabbour*

RIGHT: Marigolds are a great example of natural pest control. Farmers have been using them for years because their strong scent is said to repel pests that threaten the garden both above and below the soil, from deer to nematodes. *Bren Haas*

GALVANIZED STEEL AND WOOD CONTAINER

Designed by Scott McKinnon
Photography by Donna Griffith
Illustration by Len Churchill
Corrugated steel sheets courtesy of Conquest Steel;
shot on location at the Toronto Botanical Garden

There's something very modern-looking about galvanized steel paired with wood, especially once the wood is stained. For this project, corrugated steel sheets have been inlaid into a wooden frame, but they could just as easily be incorporated into a raised bed. This planter is the perfect size to tuck into a sunny corner of a patio or balcony. Wheels make it easy to move the container around with the sun—or into storage for the winter.

Galvanized steel sheets can be purchased from both metal companies and home centers. They're made to weather the elements. Just be careful when transporting and handling the material during construction. Wear a thick pair of work gloves when holding steel sheets because the edges can be very sharp. Usually there's only one top finished edge that isn't hazardous to your hands. Use similar caution when working in the soil around the edges of any finished raised bed that's built using these sheets. You may want to line your container with heavy plastic or cover the sharp edges with some type of material to provide a layer of protection.

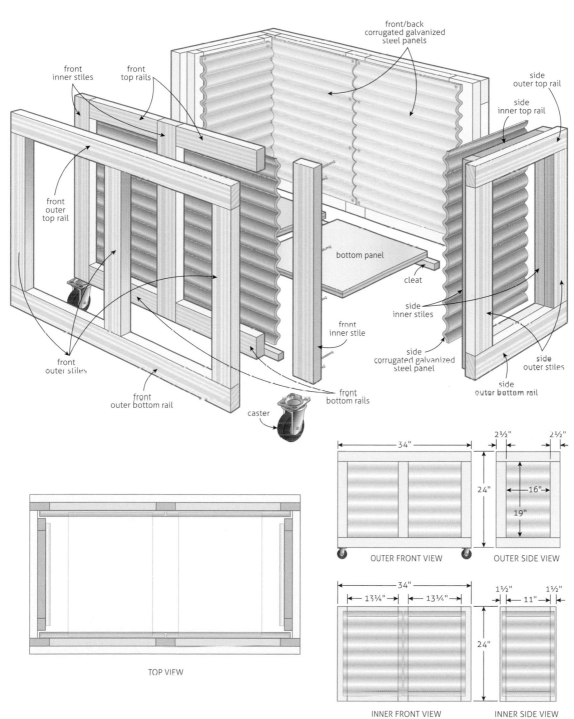

front inner stiles

front top rails

front/back
corrugated galvanized
steel panels

side
outer top rail

side
inner top rail

front
outer
top rail

bottom panel

cleat

side
inner stiles

front
inner stile

side
corrugated galvanized
steel panel

side
outer stiles

front
outer stiles

side
outer bottom rail

front
outer bottom rail

front
bottom rails

caster

TOP VIEW

2½" 2½"

34"

24"

16"

19"

OUTER FRONT VIEW

OUTER SIDE VIEW

34"

13¼" 13¼"

1½" 1½"

11"

24"

INNER FRONT VIEW

INNER SIDE VIEW

Tools

- Miter saw
- Power drill or impact driver
- Screwdriver (optional)
- Eye and ear protection
- Work gloves

Materials

- (3) 1 ×12"× 8' knotty pine boards (thickness is about 1")
- (2) 14 × 22" galvanized corrugated steel panels
- (4) 16 × 22" galvanized corrugated steel panels
- Exterior brass or anodized construction screws (¾", 1½")
- (4) 2" locking casters
- Scraps to create the removable slats along the bottom

Cut list

PART	DIMENSION	PCS
Frame, side pieces	1½ × 9¼ × 45"	2
Front and back panels	¾ × 2½ × 24"	6
Front and back panels	¾ × 2½ × 13¼"	8
Front and back panels	¾ × 2½ × 34"	4
Front and back panels	¾ × 2½ × 19"	6
End pieces	¾ × 2½ × 16"	4
End pieces	¾ × 2½ × 19"	4
End pieces	¾ × 1½ × 24"	4
End pieces	¾ × 2½ × 11"	4
Cleats	¾ × ¾ × 31½"	2
Bottom slats (measure from scrap)		

TO MAKE THE
GALVANIZED STEEL AND WOOD CONTAINER

1

2

STEP 1: START THE FRONT AND BACK PANELS.

To create the front panel, lay out the three 2½ × 24-inch pieces in a row, and place the four 2½ × 13¼-inch pieces horizontally between them. Be sure that all edges and corners are lined up. These pieces will be facing the inside of the planter.

STEP 2: ADD REINFORCEMENTS AND BUILD THE SIDE PIECES.

On top of this layout, place the 2½ × 34-inch pieces horizontally along the top and bottom and then three 2½ × 19-inch pieces on the ends and in the middle. Attach with screws. This is the outside-facing front and back of the planter. Repeat these steps to make the back panel.

To make the end pieces, lay the 16-inch pieces horizontally with two 19-inch pieces between them for the vertical pieces. On top of this frame, lay the 1½ × 24-inch pieces vertically along the inside edge of the frame, leaving an equal amount of space on either side. This is to accommodate the front and back panels during assembly. Place the 11-inch pieces horizontally between them across the top and bottom. Attach with screws.

STEP 3: POSITION THE METAL SHEETS.
Lay the 16-inch pieces of corrugated metal on top of the openings on the inside of the front and back panels.

STEP 4: ATTACH THE METAL.
Predrill holes using a ⅛ or ³⁄₁₆-inch high-speed steel (HSS) bit. Fasten the metal to the wood using ¾-inch screws. Repeat for the side panels using the 14-inch pieces of metal.

5

STEP 5: PUT THE BOX TOGETHER.
On your work surface, place a front panel perpendicular to the corner of a side panel and drill the two pieces together using 1½-inch screws. Repeat for all sides. Note that the narrower vertical strips on the inside of the end panels will allow the corners to come together more closely.

Add a shelf for the false bottom.

Cut two pieces of wood for the cleats that are ¾ × ¾ × 31½ inches. Turn the box upside down and attach the cleats with 1½-inch screws flush with the bottom of the long sides. Then nail them flush with the inside of the bottom of the panels. Use three planks measured and cut from the remaining knotty pine to rest on top of them. It's okay if there are small gaps between the slats because this is an essential part of allowing water to drain from the planter.

6

STEP 6: PUT THE BOX ON WHEELS.

Turn the project over and attach the casters with the screws that came with your casters (or ones purchased to fit them).

(See False-Bottom Fakery, page 240, to discover how you can avoid filling this entire planter with soil.)

The outside of the container was finished with a solid waterborne exterior stain. Admittedly, it might be easier to paint your pieces before putting the project together!

This planter is essentially bottomless until you install cleats onto which you can rest three removable slats cut from the remaining lumber. This allows water to drain out the bottom. The slats also can be easily replaced if they eventually succumb to rot, without having to take the entire planter apart. Furthermore, if the plan is for the planter to sit right on the ground, you actually don't have to add in a bottom at all.

This planter is rather heavy once it's been built, so the addition of rolling and locking casters means it can easily be rolled into a shed or garage, or onto a dolly, when you're placing it into storage for the winter.

PLANT IT!

While this utilitarian-chic raised bed would be perfect for growing edibles, this particular one was filled with plants chosen specifically to lure pollinators and good bugs into the garden. Here are pollinator-friendly plants that you see in the main project photo:

- Purple alyssum (*Lobularia maritime*)
- Summer savory herb
- 'Mesa Yellow' blanket flower (*Gaillardia* hybrid)
- Russian sage (*Perovskia atriplicifolia*)
- 'Peachie's Pick' Stokes' aster
- Gayfeather (*Liatris spicata*)
- Coreopsis
- Black-eyed Susan

BELOW: Many think that the term *pollinator* only refers to honeybees, but in fact there are many different pollinators that might visit your raised beds. Butterflies, hummingbirds, bats, and beetles also do the important task of pollinating plants. *Paul Zammit*

UPCYCLED SUITCASE PLANTER WITH GAS PIPE LEGS

Designed by Scott McKinnon
Photography by Donna Griffith
Illustration by Len Churchill

Antique markets and yard sales can be a treasure trove of innovative raised bed ideas. This project gave new purpose to an old wooden suitcase by transforming it into a small raised bed. Legs made from pieces of threaded gas pipe give it a modern touch. This little garden would make a perfect addition to a small patio or balcony. It's kind of like a window box without the window needing to be there.

Any wooden box will do—you can also keep an eye out for wooden wine or apple crates. And if you don't happen to have an old suitcase or box of some type, you could easily whip one together.

The suitcase planter pictured here has been filled with both edibles and ornamentals, so it's not only pretty, it's practical—and delicious!

Tools

- Screwdriver, power drill or impact driver
- Tape measure
- Old rag to handle gas pipe parts
- Eye protection
- Work gloves

Materials

FOR THE TOP:

- Shallow wooden box (we used an old suitcase about 24¼ × 17¾ × 5⅝")

FOR THE LEGS:

- ½" threaded black gas pipe (this is the pipe that's generally used to transport natural or propane gas from the street to a house) was used for this project. You could use a different width for a chunkier look, depending on the aesthetic you want.
- (4) floor/wall flanges
- (4) end caps (for the feet)
- 6½" tee fittings
- 1½" union (middle)
- (4) 24" pieces pipe threaded on each end
- (6) 6" pieces threaded pipe (also called pipe nipples)
- (4) 3½" pieces threaded pipe (also called pipe nipples)
- (16) screws (length depends on the thickness of the wood; we used #10 × ½" but could use longer if you have thicker wood)

Note: You may choose to use a bigger or smaller box. With different dimensions, you may choose to use different pipe lengths and diameters.

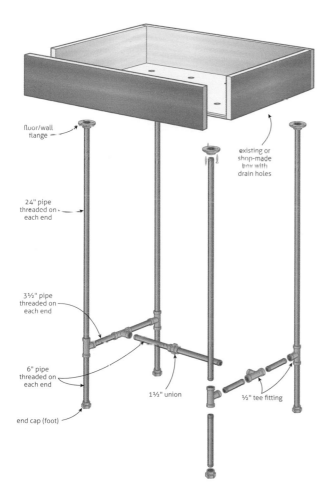

floor/wall flange

existing or shop-made box with drain holes

24" pipe threaded on each end

3½" pipe threaded on each end

6" pipe threaded on each end

1½" union

½" tee fitting

end cap (foot)

HOW TO MAKE A
UPCYCLED SUITCASE PLANTER
WITH GAS PIPE LEGS

STEP 1: PREP THE BOX.

Prepare the box that will rest on top of the gas pipe legs. Here, the top of the suitcase was removed simply by unscrewing part of the hinge. The hinges were left on the actual box as decoration.

STEP 2: DRILL DRAINAGE HOLES.

Add holes to the bottom of your box. Lay it aside for now.

STEP 3: ASSEMBLE ALL PIPE PIECES.

Have a rag close at hand as you put the gas pipe parts together; they can be quite greasy.

Screw one flange into one end of each 24-inch pipe. On the other end, add a tee fitting.

To continue the leg, add one 6-inch pipe to the opposite end of the tee. To the end of that, screw on the end cap. To the perpendicular end of the tee, add a 3½-inch threaded pipe. Repeat for the three other legs.

Use a tee to connect each set of end legs. Your project should now be in two pieces. Attach the two sets of end legs by screwing the 6-inch pieces of pipe to the middle tees of the two leg sets so they'll be parallel to the ground. Attach them with one union. It will take a bit of maneuvering to twist everything so it's just so and the feet rest on the ground evenly.

STEP 4: DETERMINE THE PERFECT LEG PLACEMENT ON THE BOX.

Set the whole leg construction with the flanges touching the box, and measure where they will go so you can screw them in place.

STEP 5: ASSEMBLE THE TOP AND BOTTOM.

Attach the flanges to the box with screws. When you turn it back over, the box can be leveled by twisting various sections of pipe as needed to make it longer or shorter.

Line the box with landscape fabric; fill with soil to prepare it for planting.

FINISHING THE LEGS

When left outdoors, the gas pipe legs will develop a natural rust-colored patina. Be careful where you place the new raised bed, however, because you don't want the rust to leach onto the surface. To protect the gas pipe legs from rusting, apply a couple of coats of tung oil (a food-grade oil) with a brush or a rag, wiping it off between coats. You could also use a rustproof spray paint— either a clear coat or a vibrant color.

PLANT IT!

This suitcase container contains a mix of edibles and ornamentals. Edibles have been used for their foliage, but they also can be snipped (herbs benefit from a regular trim) and added to summer recipes. The ornamentals add that wow factor—as both a thriller and a spiller—that you would find in a typical container arrangement. The prolific flowers you see along the front are Supertunia® Pink Star Charm petunias (no deadheading* required!), and the herbs include lemongrass, chives, rosemary, and sage, with a colorful chard added to the mix.

*Deadheading is the term used to describe the act of removing spent blooms from plants. This usually encourages more blooms to grow so the plant remains showy for longer. Some plants, however, like these Supertunias® and calibrachoas, another similar-looking annual, deadhead themselves, so no maintenance is generally required (unless they become leggy in the hot, dry heat of summer; at that point you can cut them back a bit to thicken them out as they grow back in).

CREATE A MINI BOG GARDEN IN A STOCK TANK

Designed by Jon Carloftis
Photography by Proven Winners

Stock tanks are a great vessel to use for growing water plants. They provide a ready-made, ideal container that can double as a water garden. The bog garden pictured here was created out of a 2 × 2 × 3-foot stock tank. The plug was left in and gravel was added to the bottom third of the tank. The tank was then filled with 30 percent sand and 70 percent peat and compost. Water was added to soak the soil, which was then allowed to settle before adding the plants.

It's important to note that once plants are added to a bog garden, the soil needs to remain moist at all times in order for these water-lovers to thrive.

At the nursery, look for bog plants to fill your mini pond. The ones used for this project include a selection of graceful grasses—'Baby Tut', 'King Tut', 'Blue Mohawk', fiber-optic—elephant ear, and Louisiana iris.

Refer to the section on stock tanks on page 238 for more tips on using these types of containers as raised beds.

A QUICK VERTICAL GARDENING PALLET PROJECT

Pallets have really proven their versatility in the last few years, becoming one of the most popular items that creative DIYers refurbish into a variety of household pieces. Some construction sites and even stores that get big shipments give them away for free, while others have tried to cash in on the humble pallet's popularity by charging for them. Pallets have been reimagined into everything from coffee tables and outdoor sofas to vertical gardens, which can technically be categorized as a type of raised bed, like the one shown here. Even some of the wood strips that you'll see on our Raised Bed with Upcycled Wood Design (page 100) came from pallets that had been taken apart.

Built to withstand extreme weight, pallets are generally made from hardwoods. When sourcing pallets for a project, be mindful of where you get them—you want to make sure they haven't been subjected to any toxic chemicals. Look for the letters HT, which stands for heat-treated (instead of chemical-treated). But avoid the letters MB because that means the pallet has been fumigated with methyl bromide. Avoid pallets with warped wood or cracked edges, or that look as though they've

Not only can pallets be used for practical purposes, they can be great ornamental features in a garden, as well.
Tara Nolan

been painted or stained. You don't want anything leaching into your garden, especially if you're growing food. If you're unsure, stick to planting ornamentals in your vertical garden.

Prepare your pallet by cleaning it and reattaching any loose boards. Sand all the rough sides and edges on the outward-facing side with 80-grit sandpaper attached to an orbital sander.

If your pallet has open spaces along what will be the back side, you can use a staple gun and stainless-steel staples to attach a piece of hardware cloth to it so that soil cannot escape.

If the pallet is really open along the front-facing side, create pockets with the landscape fabric, or you can use 2 × 2s to create shelves that are attached to the lower edge of each slat. The one area you want to ensure is covered is the bottom.

To plant your pallet, lay it out flat on the ground and fill with soil. Add your plants, being sure to place them close together. Water everything thoroughly. Then leave the pallet on its side for a few days to allow the roots to grow; this will help the soil stay in place when you pick it up and lean it where it's going to stay.

4 EDIBLES THAT GROW WELL IN A PALLET GARDEN

Lettuces work well in a pallet for the same reason that they work well in a lettuce table: they have shallow root systems. Choose a mix of leafy greens for a flavorful salad mix.

A medley of herbs, from thyme and oregano to chives and parsley, will do well planted within the spaces of a pallet.

Nasturtiums also make great pallet plants because they will cascade over the sides as the season progresses. Both the blooms and leaves are edible!

Strawberry plants produce runners that will also spill over the sides of a pallet.

WASHBASIN ON SAWHORSE LEGS

*Designed by Tara Nolan
and William Nolan*

It's not uncommon for gardeners to salvage old items and repurpose them as quirky garden art. This project goes a step further by reimagining an old item into an actual garden. Antique markets and yard sales are ideal places to hunt for old washbasins that can be turned into raised beds. The old metal washbasin chosen for this project was 9 inches high, a depth that made it a good candidate for growing small root vegetables. You won't get a massive crop in a container this size, but you will be able to pull a modest-sized harvest that will last you a few meals—or provide healthy snacks.

But that's not where this project ended. Rather than place the washbasin directly on the ground, it's been raised up to around waist height by using another popular DIY item: sawhorse legs. The ones used for this project are old with brackets that have aged to a nice patina. Just a little bit of work was done to create a stable platform on which the soil- and plant-laden washbasin could sit. The result? A ready-made plant stand.

BUILD IT

HOW TO MAKE A
WASHBASIN
ON SAWHORSE LEGS

- -

Tools

- Drill with a high-speed steel (HSS) drill bit
- Screws
- Eye and ear protection
- Work gloves

Materials

- Metal washbasin
- (2) Sawhorses
- Scrap wood for reinforcing (we used a piece of 2 × 4 and a piece of plywood)

STEP 1: DRILL DRAINAGE HOLES.
Drill several holes into the bottom of the basin.

STEP 2: POSITION THE LEGS.
Place the sawhorse legs where you're going to keep the raised bed. It's better to build everything on site because the washbasin will get quite heavy and hard to move once it's filled with soil.

STEP 3: ADD SUPPORT.
Depending on the sturdiness of the legs and the size of the washbasin, you may want to add a layer of support on top of the sawhorse brackets to support the washbasin (or whatever it is you place on top). Here, a scrap piece of 2 × 4 is attached with screws through the premade holes in the sawhorse bracket. Then a piece of plywood is fastened to the ends of the 2 × 4 from between the brackets, so that the basin has a sturdy place to sit. Depending on the dimensions of your washbasin, you could add extra stability by securing the washbasin directly to the plywood and then filling it with soil.

PLANT IT!

When planting from seed, keep an eye on how crowded your seedlings are once they start to poke up through the soil. As painful as it may be to throw away a baby plant, root vegetables need space around them to grow under the soil. So if the young plants are too close together, use your fingers or tweezers to gently pull the extraneous sprouts out of the soil and toss them in the compost. Beet sprouts are quite tasty, so those can just be rinsed and tossed in a salad.

This is what was planted in the washbasin pictured here:

• Early Wonder Tall Top beets
• Romeo baby carrots
• White Icicle radish
• Red-Cored Chantenay carrot
• Rainbow Swiss chard
• Leaf lettuce

Lettuce and chard will last a bit longer because it can be trimmed and used as needed, and then new growth keeps providing fresh leaves.

Cool-weather crops, such as beets, parsnips, and radishes, can be sown in early spring before the soil has completely warmed up. They can also be sown in late summer as a fall crop. That means you can enjoy fresh veggies sooner—and later—in the season.
Tara Nolan

TIPS FOR ADDING RAISED BEDS TO A BALCONY OR ROOFTOP PATIO

Having a small space does not put you at a disadvantage. You can still have a garden that yields a decent harvest yet goes beyond the basics of a couple of herbs and a tomato plant. You just need to get creative with your space.

Will there be challenges? Yes. However, there are some advantages too. For example, you won't attract the same level of pests that can attack plants in a backyard garden—at least nothing of the four-legged variety. You won't be totally immune to insect pests, but there shouldn't be as many to contend with. Unfortunately your garden will not benefit from the good guys, like worms. And, because you are creating a self-contained eco-system, you will need to replenish your soil more often. New soil should be used every year.

© Les Urbainculteurs / Smart Pots

If your balcony or rooftop patio gets six to eight hours of sunshine a day, you're in luck because you can tick "proper growing conditions" off your list of planting requirements. All you need is a raised bed—albeit one that is more compact—that fits into your small space.

Balconies are built to withstand extra weight from people, snow load, and so on, but to minimize putting added stress on a balcony, opt for lightweight materials for your raised bed, and choose soil mixes that are fluffy. Compressed mixes exist specifically for these types of gardens. If you're building from a kit, look for a light, modular one that can easily be built on-site.

There are, however, a few elements that will differ when you're gardening several floors up rather than on terra firma. First and foremost, you can't toss everything into a wheelbarrow or make several trips back and forth to the backyard from the car. You're likely dealing with an elevator—or

© Les Urbainculteurs / Smart Pots

maybe even stairs. Consider what you have to lug up and down, what you may have to store over the winter, as well as the fact that you'll be carrying all your materials, plants, and soil through your apartment or condo.

Here are a few more things to take into consideration when you're planting in the sky.

READ YOUR BUILDING'S RULES

Before you invest time and money into a garden, carefully read the legal and safety requirements for your building. You need to consider the weight of your raised beds once they're full of soil as well as drainage issues. Avoid heavy materials like concrete.

Keep in mind that terraces may be considered a common element, meaning that the building owns the outdoor space and the owner has the exclusive usage rights to it. Your setup, whatever it may be, should have zero impact on the building.

Most regulations emphasize that you should not install a planter that someone could technically step up on, putting them in danger if it's close to a balcony railing. Consult with your building management if you're not sure what's permitted and what is not.

CONSIDER THE ELEMENTS

If you're on a balcony that's covered, you may get the intense sun, but your plants may not benefit from a good rainstorm as they would in the garden (depending on the direction of the rain).

Wind, on the other hand, can reach your plants, wherever they are. Wind can be incredibly drying, and it can also wreak havoc on delicate plants. In some instances, a strong wind current could lift the soil right out of the planter! If your space tends to be windy, you may need to think of using some type of windbreak to protect your plants.

Direct sun can be much harsher on a balcony or rooftop, as well, so creating a bit of shade may work to your advantage.

CHECK ZONING LAWS

Depending on how big your balcony garden will be, you may want to check not only your building regulations but also zoning laws, or even an architect, to assess the impact of the weight of your garden.

DEVISE A WATERING PLAN

Keep in mind that during the steamy summer months, gardens can dry out quickly in the hot sun, so some containers may need to be watered twice a day.

Most balconies don't have the luxury of access to an outdoor tap so you may want to consider a watering setup that has a built-in reservoir.

On a roof, a small holding tank could be used to store rainwater that is then distributed to the plants via a dripline irrigation system.

Drainage is important, but you want to make sure any overflow isn't dripping onto a neighbor's space. You can use small trays with planters that don't have a built-in reservoir to hold water.

Fabric pots are also an option because they drain well and provide good aeration around the roots (for examples, see Chapter 6: Not Handy? No Problem!, page 235).

MASTER THE FALSE BOTTOM

Depending on the size of the raised bed you place on your balcony or rooftop, keep in mind that you don't need to fill the entire thing with soil. Packing peanuts, for example, make good space fillers. They're light and readily available, and water drains through them easily.

Another way to take up space in your planter is to line the sides with Styrofoam or ¼-inch insulation sheets. Just be sure to line the sides with landscape fabric first.

And there's a bonus to lining the sides of your balcony-sized raised bed: if you happen to leave it outdoors over the winter and the soil freezes solid, it won't split open the sides.

(See False-Bottom Fakery, page 240, for more tips.)

PLANT IT!

While you may think that certain edibles are off-limits for balcony or rooftop gardens—pumpkins, melons, and so on—there are varieties of plants that are more compact, making them perfect for small spaces. Even tomatoes come in patio varieties, meaning you won't be struggling to contain a monster plant.

When you're on the hunt for seeds or plants, keep your eyes open for these varieties:

- Tumbling Tom tomato
- Sweet 'n' Neat cherry tomato
- Yellow Canary tomato
- Window Box Roma tomato
- Patio Snacker cucumber
- Tom Thumb pea (patio variety)
- Redskin F1 pepper
- Snackbite pepper

Some companies, such as Renee's Garden Seeds, offer patio collections, which are bundled packets of seeds tailored especially for those with small spaces. Renee's sells a package that includes lettuce, basil, nasturtiums, tomatoes, and radishes.

GROWING VERTICALLY

Growing up is a smart way to maximize space, especially when you don't have much space to work with in the first place. Training plants up a trellis certainly helps as you can pack more into the garden. But you can also garden on a wall.

When the vertical gardening trend first appeared, kits and materials were only available to tradespeople who would use them to cover entire walls. Then easy-to-assemble consumer-ready kits started popping up in garden centers, nurseries, and home centers.

Small edibles, such as herbs and lettuces, are already small enough for balcony gardens, but many larger plants, such as tomatoes and melons, come in compact varieties that fit perfectly in small spaces.

Many gardeners use vertical gardens more as ornamental containers, full of lush foliage and beautiful blooms. Members of the sedum family are popular because they're drought-resistant and can tolerate hot sun.

However, more and more clever green thumbs are using vertical gardens to grow food, whether it's a few herbs, some greens, or edible flowers.

Check the rules. If you're in a condo or an apartment, you should look over your regulations to ensure that you're allowed to hang things from the outdoor walls.

Consider watering needs. Plants grown vertically are sitting in less soil and tend to dry out more quickly, so they need to be watered often. A dripline system could take care of this task, but many vertical planters do come with reservoirs that store and distribute water as needed.

HOW A ROOFTOP EXPERIMENT ENDED IN SUCCESS— AND A PRESTIGIOUS AWARD

When Johanne Daoust started gardening in 2004, she planted in a few 5-gallon pails that she sat atop the 430-square-foot rooftop of her 100-year-old home. Then she read about Square Foot Gardening at a friend's cottage and wanted to try out that method for herself. So her partner built six raised beds that were 2 feet wide by 4 feet long and 8 inches deep. They were conventional beds made out of cedar with holes in the bottom.

Daoust's next gardening experiment came in the form of the framing system that she installed to protect her plants from unscrupulous raccoons, squirrels, and birds. After that addition, Daoust realized that when she watered, a great deal of runoff cascaded off the roof and onto the ground below. "I thought, there's got to be a better way to save this water," she says. "I wanted to be able to conserve it." When tomatoes are in full bloom in the heat of the summer, they can take up to a gallon of water a day, so you have to water twice a day.

That winter, Daoust spent time researching online and discovered subirrigation expert Bob Hyland. He had worked a lot designing subirrigated planters (SIPs) for indoor plants. Not only did Daoust pore over his archives, she tracked him down and asked him questions, which resulted in her developing her own subirrigated planter system that she has perfected over time and still uses to this day. Basically, the water is introduced from the bottom (via a fill tube) in a SIP, where it's soaked upward toward the plant rather than from the top (which is what happens when you water a plant the traditional way).

Once spring arrived, Daoust thought she would convert one of her beds to her new SIP system, but she ended up converting the whole garden. She put plastic liner in all the pots and raised beds—to cover holes—and sank the oxygen reservoir in the

TOP: Each year, Johanne Daoust hosts workshops so that she can pass on her knowledge. "I'm interested in the complete process and the system of growing and making it available to people. I believe you can grow food wherever you are and with however much space you have." *Tara Nolan*

MIDDLE LEFT: You have the option of making your own SIP or buying one from renowned companies like Lechuza. Johanne Daoust has made many of her own, but she likes to test out the new ones that come on the market. *Tara Nolan*

MIDDLE RIGHT: To make her own SIP system, Johanne Daoust will put a nylon stocking over a piece of corrugated perforated drainage tube. (The stocking prevents the plant roots from growing into the perforations.) She will either line up a few so they cover the bottom of a raised bed, or she'll snake one along the bottom and bring it up to the top of the SIP, so that it also acts as the SIP's fill tube. She'll also use stacked water bottles that attach directly to the oxygen chamber as the fill tube. *Tara Nolan*

BOTTOM: Even fabric pots get the SIP treatment on Johanne Daoust's rooftop garden. *Johanne Daoust*

bottom. Then she used a perforated pipe system to create her SIP. "The first one I found was on my neighbor's reno debris pile," she says.

Now each raised bed has the special framing system on top and the subirrigation system in the bottom. Those in the rooftop gardening industry have taken notice. Daoust headed to New York to collect an award from Green Roofs for Healthy Cities in 2015.

Daoust has been teaching graphic design courses at a local college for 26 years. One of those courses, Design Thinking, is the process Daoust uses to problem-solve in her garden. "I learned by observation, I learned by doing, and I learned by failure."

HOW DOES IT WORK?
In a subirrigated planter, there's an oxygen water chamber in the bottom of the pot where the soil and water meet; capillary action wicks water up through the soil. Plant roots get both water and oxygen, so it becomes an optimal growing system.

SITUATING THE BEDS
Daoust highly recommends making an appointment with a structural engineer to tell you how much weight your roof can hold before you set up shop with any raised beds. She carefully positioned her raised beds to distribute the weight.

Daoust's raised beds sit on 2 inches of blue insulation Styrofoam. This prevents the beds from digging into the surface of the roof.

In the winter, Daoust covers everything so that they don't fill up with snow and then crack. Trellises are laid down on the roof and covered with plastic so they're protected.

Subirrigated planters have to be level so that the water doesn't drain into one area. "I spend a lot of time re-leveling pots and raised beds," says Daoust.

WHAT SHE GROWS
- Arugula
- Beans (different kinds of runner beans that climb 6-foot trellises)
- Butternut squash
- Cantaloupe
- Cucumbers
- Eggplant (two types)
- French garden beans (a bush variety)
- Herbs (basil—11 containers, compact thyme—a favorite because it forms a ball that's really good for containers, oregano, rosemary, sage, thyme)
- Leeks in fabric grow bags
- Onions
- Peas
- Peppers (sweet and hot)
- Tomatoes (17 varieties of heirlooms)
- Zucchini

Some of the benefits of Daoust's subirrigated planter system include:

- You can extend the season. Daoust starts to garden in March because each bed becomes like a mini greenhouse.
- During the growing season, Daoust protects certain plants with shade cloth. "Even plants that like heat can get sun-scalded," she says. The shade cloth knocks the temperature down by 50 percent. "I can grow lettuce all summer without it bolting."
- Wire mesh prevents the squirrels and raccoons from getting in.
- Frames come apart easily in the fall for winter storage and are laid out flat on the roof.
- Each system has an overflow hole, so water drains out if there's excessive rainfall. "It's like your safety valve," explains Daoust.

CHAPTER 5

RAISED BEDS WITH PURPOSE

There's no denying that all raised beds are built with a purpose in mind. But the ones in this chapter go a step further from the typical raised bed in their function and utility. While raised beds are versatile enough that you can pretty much grow anything in them, the beds in this chapter tend to have more of a singular purpose.

For those who want to test their green thumb growing spuds, a stackable potato bin makes it especially easy for first-timers.

Season extenders figure into this purpose-driven chapter with a cleverly constructed greenhouse that fits right over a raised bed and a cold frame made from an upcycled window that dispels the notion that there is only one growing season. They can both be used to harden off seedlings, store plants that need to go dormant, and extend the season, allowing fresh greens and root veggies to be picked during the winter months.

Speaking of fresh greens, the lettuce table in this chapter was created from a repurposed antique. This can be tucked into the corner of a small patio, balcony, or deck and provide instant salads made from a mixture of greens. Don't be afraid to experiment with pea shoots, baby amaranth leaves, and different varieties of lettuces and greens.

Rolling casters, as exemplified on a Versailles-inspired raised bed, are a boon to gardeners, allowing them to freely move plants into sunlight, storage, or wherever it is they need to go.

There are a few other inspiring ideas with unique purposes to be discovered. Hopefully it sparks your imagination to add some raised beds that will take your garden to the next level.

RIGHT: Raised beds are for the birds: this raised bed garden atop a chicken coop takes raised bed gardening to a new level. You can see that a variety of edible flowers and greens have been planted in the shallow rooftop garden. Do the chickens approve? *Tara Nolan*

BELOW: Binder clips and bricks are used to secure the row cover that's protecting this raised bed. *Niki Jabbour*

BELOW RIGHT: Rocks and spring clamps hold a "row cover"—in this case, it's a clear plastic painting dropcloth—in place to keep the cold out and get a head start on germination. Gardener Meighan Makarchuk describes it as "inexpensive and effective." *Meighan Makarchuk*

ABOVE: Bricks and mortar provide a thick, solid, cozy foundation for a cold frame.

ABOVE LEFT: Corrugated plastic can be used to fill in the sides of a cold frame and capture light and heat from all directions.

LEFT: Lettuce tables are a great way to ensure you're picking your salads fresh from the garden. Place one right out your back door or on a balcony for easy access. *University of Maryland Extension*

BOTTOM: All the edibles grown in these raised beds are grown for food banks and education programs. *Alex Rochon-Terry*

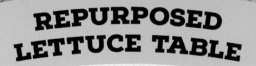

REPURPOSED
LETTUCE TABLE

Designed by Tara Nolan
Photography by Donna Griffith

For many, salads are a staple side dish at every meal, especially throughout the summer! For others, they are *the* meal. Imagine stepping out your door with a pair of scissors in hand, ready to snip a fresh salad.

Enter the lettuce table: a raised bed with a depth that's shallower than your standard raised garden. This table is perfect for greens that are shallow-rooted because they don't need as much depth to grow lush and full.

There are lots of plans out there for basic frames, but for this project, I wanted something that had fancy legs. Browsing around a local antique market, there were lots of options, from old desks (you could use the top and pull out the drawers as mini gardens!) to mix-and-match legs that you could attach to the top of your choosing. But then I happened upon this small, antique kitchen table and fell in love with the shape. The top was not attached, which made my project even easier. My original plan was to build a separate lettuce table frame to lay over the antique table, but then I realized I could use the table itself as the frame.

There are many benefits to planting a lettuce table:

- It's compact and can easily be moved around. In the summer, when lettuce likes to bolt, you can move it to a shadier spot.

- Raising your garden up high means bunnies and groundhogs and other lettuce-lovers won't be hopping in for a nibble.

- A mesh bottom allows for quick and easy drainage.

- Greens don't mind cooler weather—in fact, they thrive in it—so you can start fresh greens early in the spring and enjoy them right through to the fall.

Tools

- Drill/driver or screwdriver
- Tin snips or wire cutters
- Tape measure
- Handsaw or miter saw
- Eye and ear protection
- Work gloves

Materials

- An old table or desk
- Small nails
- Hardware cloth (looks like a very fine chicken wire)
- Landscape fabric
- Protective gloves
- Thin cedar lattice (for this project, we used lattice that's roughly 1½" wide and ⅜" thick)

HOW TO MAKE A
REPURPOSED LETTUCE TABLE

1

STEP 1: Flip the table upside down and place it on a workbench. With gloves on, cut the hardware cloth to size with wire cutters or tin snips.

STEP 2: Stretch the hardware cloth over the frame; hold it in place with small nails. (This might be a two-person job, depending on the size of the table. Just make sure you're both wearing gloves.)

STEP 3: Cut the cedar lattice to the size of the table frame so that it covers the ends of the hardware cloth; nail the lattice in place around the undersides of the table with small nails. This will doubly secure the hardware cloth. Depending on the size of your table, you may also want to create a support beam across the middle.

STEP 4: Take a quick peek to ensure there is no hardware cloth peeking out from under the lattice strips. Snip off any overhang.

STEP 5: Turn the table back over and line the bottom of it with landscape fabric.

STEP 6: Fill your with soil and plant.

PLANT IT!

There's nothing as satisfying as snipping your own fresh salad mix for dinner. *Niki Jabbour*

- Stagger your seed planting by a few days so that you have continuous crops.
- Plant more than one variety for interesting salads.
- Snip lettuce regularly to stimulate new leaf growth.
- When the lettuce starts to bolt, pull it out and toss it in the compost.

Don't just stick to lettuce. For flavorful, interesting salads, choose a variety of greens to plant, from Asian varieties (mizuna, tatsoi, bok choy) to tasty sprouts from baby plants (sunflowers, peas, beets).

Here are some varieties you might want to check out:

- Lolla Rossa Darkness lettuce
- Blush Batavian French lettuce
- Kalettes
- Gala mache
- Baby oakleaf lettuce

The greens that were used in this lettuce table project include:

- Radicchio
- Red Sails lettuce
- Baby bok choy
- Lolla Rossa Darkness lettuce
- Tuscan baby leaf kale
- Red Garnet amaranth

You can also throw in some peas to garnish salads with fresh pea shoots. When browsing seed catalogs, look for packages of salad blends that choose the varieties for you!

Toss in a couple of herbs to add another dimension of flavor to your mix of greens, including parsley, basil, and dill. These can also be used in salad dressings.

MAKING A LETTUCE TABLE FROM SCRATCH

If you don't happen to have an upcycled table that you can fashion into a lettuce table, you can make your own tray and base. Use cedar, redwood, or any other naturally rot-resistant wood for all the parts of this project. Jazz it up by using an outdoor paint or stain to give your plain lettuce table some color. Just be sure to not paint the inside edges that will touch the soil.

Photo: University of Maryland Extension

Tools

- Drill
- Miter saw
- Tin snips
- Hammer
- Caulking gun
- Clamps
- Staple gun with $5/16$" stainless-steel staples
- Countersink
- Carpenter's square
- Eye and ear protection
- Work gloves

Materials

- (2) 2 × 4" × 8' boards
- (4) 2 × 4" × 12'
- (3) 1 × 2" × 8'
- $1/4$" galvanized hardware cloth
- Landscape fabric
- Construction adhesive
- (1 lb.) $2\frac{1}{2}$" deck screws
- (1 lb.) 1" roofing nails

Cut list

PART	DIMENSION	PCS
Tray side	$1\frac{1}{2}$ × $3\frac{1}{2}$ × 72"	2
Tray ends and divider	$1\frac{1}{2}$ × $3\frac{1}{2}$ × 21"	3
Outer leg	$1\frac{1}{2}$ × $3\frac{1}{2}$ × 36"	4
Inner leg	$1\frac{1}{2}$ × $3\frac{1}{2}$ × $20\frac{1}{2}$"	4
Bottom leg	$1\frac{1}{2}$ × $3\frac{1}{2}$ × $8\frac{1}{2}$"	4
Stretcher	$1\frac{1}{2}$ × $3\frac{1}{2}$ × 69"	1
Top stretcher	$1\frac{1}{2}$ × $3\frac{1}{2}$ × 72"	1
Center support	$1\frac{1}{2}$ × $3\frac{1}{2}$ × 19"	1
Side rail	$1\frac{1}{2}$ × $3\frac{1}{2}$ × 24"	2
Side trim	$3/4$ × $1\frac{1}{2}$ × 71"	2
End trim	$3/4$ × $1\frac{1}{2}$ × 17"	2

HOW TO MAKE A
LETTUCE TABLE FROM SCRATCH

STEP 1: MAKE THE TABLE FRAME.

Cut the parts for the table frame to length, and assemble the cedar top tray with the center divider. Fasten with two deck screws at each corner (be sure to predrill all screw holes to avoid splits). This design is measured out for a 2 × 6-foot tray, but you can make it larger or smaller.

STEP 2: ATTACH THE HARDWARE CLOTH TO THE FRAME.

Wearing thick gloves, use the tin snips to cut the hardware cloth to the size of the frame. Center the cloth on the underside of the frame so that it's in ¼ inch from the edge on all sides. Cut out a 2 × 4-inch section at each corner for the legs and a 2 × 4-inch slot at the center of the divider. Use roofing nails to nail the hardware cloth in place every 6 inches on the center divider. Stretch it on each side, and nail along the ends. You don't need too many nails because you'll be covering the cloth with 1 × 2s.

STEP 3: PREPARE THE LEGS. Cut the inner and outer leg pieces, and assemble them into two leg pairs. Screw the inner and outer legs together, leaving a 3½-inch gap at the top. The top frame will sit on the ledges created at the top. Leave the bottom legs off for now. Make sure the legs are parallel to each other, and then join them together with the side rails. Spread a bead of construction adhesive before attaching the two pieces. Set the legs down parallel to each other, and join them with the side rails.

STEP 4: ATTACH THE LEGS.
With the tray turned upside down, fit the legs onto the ends. Check that they're square to the frame and sitting flat underneath it—if you see daylight between the inner leg and the tray, trim the outer leg a bit so the gap disappears. Screw each leg to both parts of the cedar frame.

STEP 5: ADD THE STRETCHER.
Fit the stretcher between the leg ends and clamp in place. Predrill holes, and then attach with screws. Measure and cut the short bottom pieces of the legs and fasten them with adhesive and screws.

STEP 6: ADD THE MIDDLE SUPPORT STRETCHER.

Place the table right-side up and screw the top stretcher to the lower one and the side rails. Measure the distance from the stretchers to the center divider (add 1/16 inch to make sure you have a snug fit) and then cut and fasten the support.

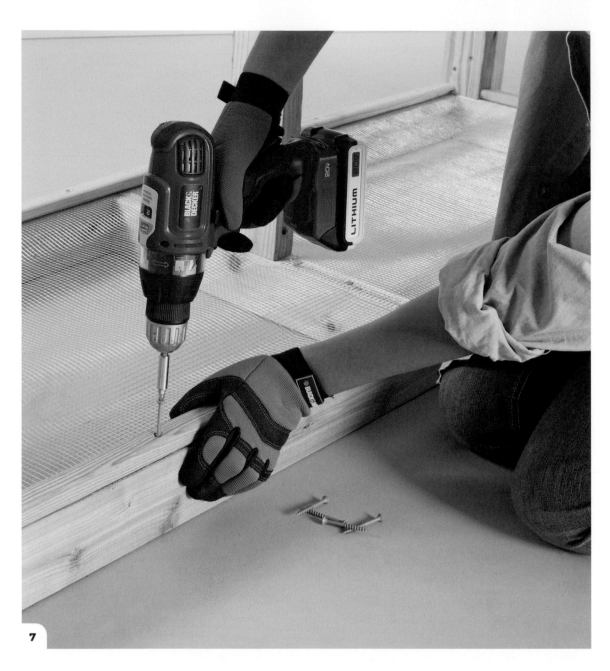

7

STEP 7: SECURE THE HARDWARE CLOTH.
Predrill the 1 × 2s every 8 to 10 inches. Flip the table upside-down, and then screw the 1 × 2 pieces to the bottom of the tray so that they're flush with the outside edges and covering the hardware cloth.

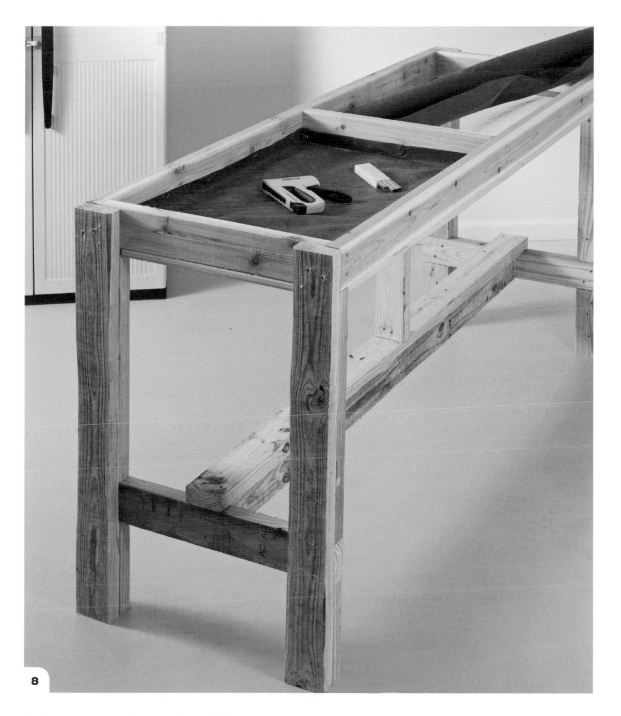

STEP 8: ADD LANDSCAPE FABRIC.
Staple the landscape fabric on the inside of the tray. This will hold the soil in place.

VERSAILLES-INSPIRED PLANTER

Designed by Scott McKinnon
Photography by Donna Griffith
Illustration by Len Churchill

The inspiration behind the design of this versatile planter has royal roots. André Le Nôtre, King Louis XIV's gardener, is said to have designed the first "Versailles planter" in 1670 for the orange trees that were imported to Versailles, France. These tropical specimens that provided fruit to the court would not have survived the winter weather in this region of France. The solution was to plant them in portable containers that could be moved from the formal gardens into a greenhouse called an "orangerie" during the coldest months of the year.

In the 1800s, the design was modernized with the addition of a cast-iron frame meant to support the weight of the trees. There were also various flourishes added, such as hinged doors and finials.

This project is more compact, perfect for a balcony or patio, or even beside the front door, though you can expand the dimensions to make something much larger. The box will accommodate a 14-inch pot planted with a small tree or shrub. The planter shown here is holding a highbush blueberry. The casters make it easy to roll the container into storage over the winter. They also keep the container off the ground. Holes could be added to the bottom if you were to plant right in the box rather than setting a pot inside.

This rolling raised bed is also handy if you happen to have a plant like a fig tree that needs to go dormant over the winter. Simply roll the container into its dark, cold storage over the winter months and then roll it back out come spring.

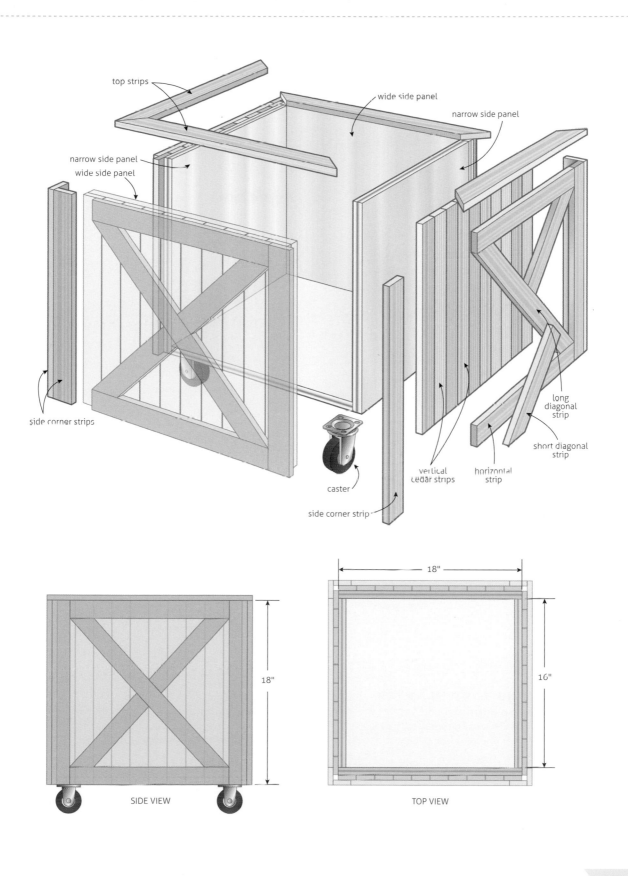

top strips

wide side panel

narrow side panel

narrow side panel

wide side panel

side corner strips

long diagonal strip

short diagonal strip

side corner strip

caster

vertical cedar strips

horizontal strip

18"

SIDE VIEW

18"

16"

TOP VIEW

Tools

- Miter saw
- Hammer or pneumatic nailer
- Sandpaper or rounding plane
- Bevel square or carpenter's square and a pencil
- Power drill or impact driver
- Eye and ear protection
- Work gloves

Materials

- (4) 2½" casters
- (1) ¾" 4' × 8' sheet exterior plywood
- (1 box) 1½" exterior screws
- (12) ½" × 1¾" × 10' cedar strips
- (1 box) Finishing nails

Cut list

PART	DIMENSION	PCS
Box side	18 × 18"	2
Box side	16½ × 18"	2
Box bottom	16½ × 16½"	1
Cedar strips	18"	48
Top edge	Measure to fit	4
"X" pattern	Measure to fit	8

PAINTING YOUR PLANTER

The fun part is choosing a color to paint your new planter. Choose an outdoor paint or stain that will also help to protect the wood. The planters outside Versailles are a greenish hue. But you could match your planter to the front door of your house or choose a really bold color that will pop wherever you choose to place it!

HOW TO MAKE A
VERSAILLES-INSPIRED PLANTER

1

2

STEP 1: CUT THE BOX PIECES.
Cut two pieces of plywood 18 × 18 inches (for side pieces) and two pieces of plywood 16½ × 18 inches (for the other side pieces). Cut one piece of plywood 16½ × 16½ inches (for the bottom). Assemble the plywood box with the smaller sides inside the larger ones, and the bottom panel enclosed on all sides. Attach with screws.

STEP 2: FINISH ALL THE EDGES.
With a rounding plane or sandpaper, round the long edges of all the cedar strips. This gives them a nice finished edge.

STEP 3: CREATE THE CEDAR STRIPS.
Cut 48 pieces of cedar strip to 18 inches each. Lay 10 pieces out per side, nailing them on vertically with finishing nails.

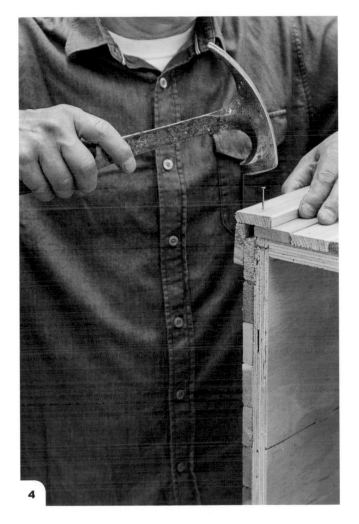

STEP 4: ATTACH THE SIDE CORNERS.
To make a side corner, place two strips
perpendicular to each other so that each piece
meets evenly at the corner of the box. They'll form
an L shape. Nail the strips tight. Repeat for all the
other corners.

Measure for the horizontal strips that run between
the corner pieces along the top and the bottom.

Note: Lapping the corners as was done in the
previous step could alter the measurements for
these pieces a little. Be sure to measure them
before cutting. Attach these eight strips (top and
bottom on all four sides) by nailing in place.

STEP 5: MAKE THE TOP OF THE BOX.

To make the top edge of the planter, start by taking a longer piece of cedar and measuring the inside lengths of the planter. This is the measurement you want so you can cut two opposing 45-degree angles on either end so all the pieces meet evenly in the corners. Continue to measure and cut all the way around. Nail everything in place.

STEP 6: MEASURE AND CUT TO FORM THE X.

Lay a piece from corner to corner, and line it up how you want in the corners. Mark with a pencil the angled cut you'll need to make it fit in. It should be 45 degrees or very close depending on how you've laid out the box. For the cross piece, mark out where it's going to need to be cut out in the center so that the two pieces fit snugly around the other half of the X. Repeat for all sides.

7

STEP 7: ADD CASTERS.

Turn the planter over, and place the casters at the edges of the plywood.

Predrill the holes for the casters' screws using a ¼-inch wood bit. Attach the casters with the screws and add a nut and bolt from the inside to secure in place.

WHAT DOES A ROUNDING PLANE DO?

To give this planter a more refined look, a mini handheld edge-rounding plane created slightly curved and smooth edges in the wood. The one used for this project could be used on the push stroke, creating the desired effect in one or two passes.

POTATO-GROWING BOX

Designed and written by Chris Peterson
Photography by Tracy Walsh
Illustration by Bill Kersey

Digging up potatoes has to be one of the most satisfying parts of the harvest. Perhaps it's because you really don't know what's happening underneath the soil until it's time to dig up your potatoes, whereas with edibles that fruit on branches, you can ascertain right away the likelihood of growing a successful crop.

For some reason, seed potatoes are not as prevalent at the local garden center in springtime as other veggies, like onions. The thing is, it's just as easy to plant potatoes as it is many of the more popular vegetables you'll find at garden centers.

The trick with growing potato plants is to build hills of soil around them as they grow. The branches you cover will produce offshoots that can also grow potatoes, meaning you'll have several levels of spuds once your crop is ready to harvest.

Admittedly, it can be hard to keep a nice, orderly pile around the potatoes. But this clever DIY potato box has levels that you can add as the season progresses and the plants grow taller, and you can keep the soil contained within. Half-lap joints allow all of the levels to fit together snugly like a puzzle. Having a potato box also means you don't have to take up space in the rest of your raised beds for your potato crop.

This special raised bed construction also makes it easier to harvest your spuds, as you simply lift off the layers one at a time (be sure to have something on hand to catch the soil) to reveal the tasty tubers.

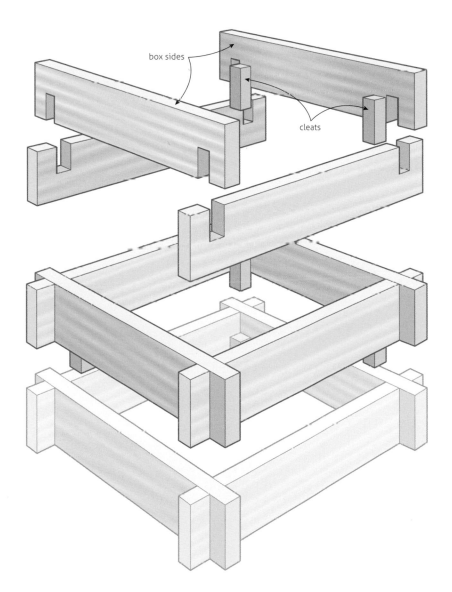

box sides

cleats

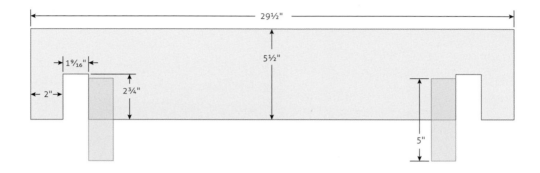

Tools

- Table saw or circular saw
- Drill
- Mallet
- Chisel
- Carpenter's square
- Tape measure
- Eye and ear protection
- Work gloves

Materials

- (5) 2" × 6" × 8'
- (1) 2 × 2 × 8'
- 2½" deck screws

Cut list

PART	DIMENSION	PCS
Box sides	1½ × 5½ × 29½"	16
Box cleats	1½ × 1½ × 5"	16

HOW TO MAKE A
POTATO-GROWING BOX

1

2

STEP 1: CUT THE BOX SIDES.

Carefully cut the sides for the box. All the pieces need to be exactly the same dimensions and the ends perfectly square. Lay out the half-lap notches on two of the boards as shown, making each 1⁹⁄₁₆ inches wide. Screw a straight board to the sliding miter gauge to keep the sides straight as you push them through. The depth of each notch is exactly half of the board's width, so measure the boards and adjust the depth as needed. Align and clamp the boards to the miter gauge. Make the first cut at 2 inches from the end, and then slide the boards over 1⁹⁄₁₆ inches and make the second cut. (You can also use a circular saw or a jigsaw to make these cuts.)

STEP 2: HONE YOUR HALF-LAP NOTCHES.

Break off the waste material and clean up the bottom of the notch with a sharp chisel. Check the fit. If everything looks good, cut the rest of the boards on the table saw. If you're using a circular saw, trace the notches onto the remaining boards with a sharp pencil and then cut out all of the remaining notches.

Note: Only the bottom layer of boards has to be the exact same depth. If it's a little deep, you can drive a screw in at the base and turn it in or out to make the top edges level.

3

4

STEP 3: PREPARE AND INSTALL THE CLEATS.

Use a square to mark positioning lines for the cleats on each board, marking the lines just to the inside of each notch. These represent the outside faces of the 2 × 2-inch cleats. Mark a vertical line 3 inches above the base of each notch; this represents the top end of each cleat. Install the cleats by drilling countersunk pilot holes, and fastening the cleats to the boards with pairs of 2½-inch deck screws.

Note: For the bottom course of the box, you can omit the cleats, if desired, or you can make longer cleats with pointed ends to help anchor the box to the ground.

STEP 4: TAKE A TEST RUN.

Test-fit the parts by assembling the entire box. Use a carpenter's square or measure diagonally between opposing corners of the box frame to make sure the frame is square. Plant your seed potatoes about four to eight inches deep, and cover with soil or mulch. As the plants spring out of the ground, add more soil and additional pieces until the box is complete.

HOW DO I KNOW
MY POTATOES ARE READY?

This is a good question because everything is happening under the soil! The rule of thumb is that potatoes are ready to be harvested once the plant has flowered and the stems start to die back. Then you can gently feel around in the soil to see if anything is ready to harvest. With this box, the task is made even easier because you can start removing the sides one by one to uncover your ready-to-eat spuds. Be careful not to bruise your harvest because they won't store for as long if they're damaged.

If you happen to be eating your potatoes right away, rinse them gently and pat dry with a tea towel. *Tara Nolan*

COLD FRAME USING AN OLD WINDOW

Designed by Deon Haupt and Tara Nolan
Photography by Donna Griffith
Illustration by Len Churchill

Have you ever picked a fresh salad during the winter solstice? Many gardeners might think that the growing season ends in autumn once the last fruits of the harvest have been picked. However, a season extender will keep green thumbs stocked with root vegetables and greens all winter long. Enter the mighty cold frame. This simple contraption has a clear glass or plastic top that harnesses the sun's winter rays, keeps plants warm enough to grow, and prevents them from freezing into ice cubes. In fact, depending on the day, it just might get too hot in there. You may need to crack the top open and let some fresh, frosty air in! An indoor/outdoor thermometer will help you keep tabs on the temperature. Also, keep in mind that after a storm, you need to make sure to clear away the snow from the lid. The result is fresh, unexpected produce throughout the winter.

For this version of a cold frame, rather than source plastic or glass to make the top, an old window was upcycled and simply attached to the bed with hinges. Old windows are usually readily found at antique stores and markets. All the measurements for this project were determined by the size of the window, which had perfect dimensions to work with when creating this small, compact cold frame.

When building the base, make sure the top level is slanted so that the top closes on an angle towards the sun. The back should be about 3 to 6 inches higher than the front. Winter sunlight is weaker, so this shape helps to capture as much solar energy as possible. Digging your cold frame into the ground by a few inches, will also add further insulation.

Fill with fresh soil, leaving space near the top, and all you need to do is figure out which seeds to plant.

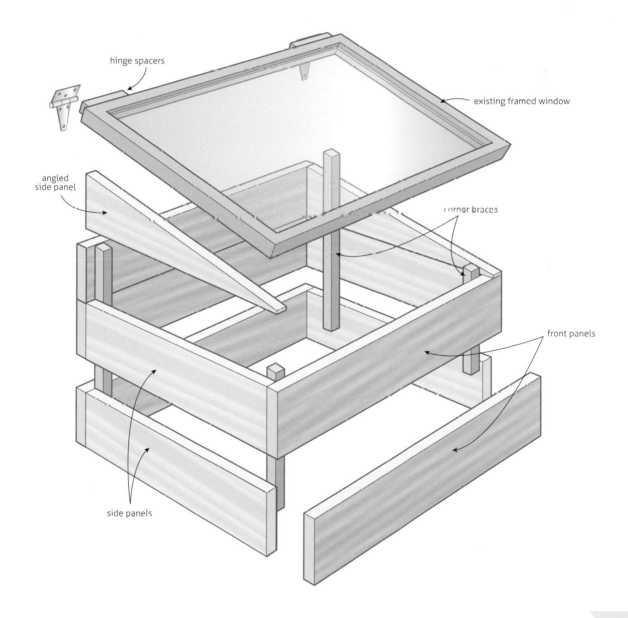

hinge spacers

existing framed window

angled side panel

corner braces

front panels

side panels

Tools

- Miter saw
- Circular saw or jigsaw
- Japanese dozuki saw
- Orbital sander or sandpaper
- Power drill or impact driver
- Straight edge and pencil
- Clamps (optional)
- Tape measure
- Eye and ear protection
- Work gloves

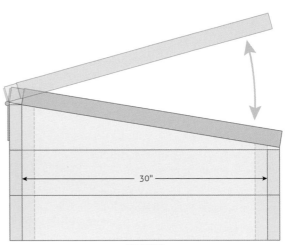

SIDE VIEW

Materials

Note: This project was made to accommodate an old window that's 32¼" long × 30" wide.

- (4) 2" × 6" × 8' cedar boards
- (2) hinges
- 2¾" screws

Cut list

PART	DIMENSION	PCS
Front and back pieces	1½ × 5½ × 32¼"	5
Side pieces	1½ × 5½ × 30"	4
Angled side pieces (see instructions)	1½ × 5½ × 30"	2
Corner braces (cut from scrap)	2½ × 6× 16½"	2
Corner braces (cut from scrap)	2½ × 6 × 11"	2

HOW TO MAKE A
COLD FRAME
USING AN OLD WINDOW

2

STEP 1: BUILD THE FRAME.

Lay out the 32¼-inch front and back pieces so that they cover the sides of the 30-inch side pieces to form a box. Screw in place to make the bottom of the frame. Repeat this step to create the second layer. For the third layer, there is a back piece but no front piece because of the angled slope you want to create once the window is attached. This means the side pieces need to be cut at an angle. They also need to be longer to accommodate the slope. Leave about 10 inches on the end in order to either screw or clamp the work piece down to your bench for when you make the cut. Screw the side piece to the back piece temporarily, and place on top of the box. Take a straight edge and place it from the edge of the top corner to the front of the box diagonally across the board and draw a line.

Remove the temporary screws and attach the extra 10-inch length to your work table with clamps or screws. Use a circular saw or jigsaw to slowly cut it out as you're going across the grain. One cut gives you both angled side pieces. Trim the extra 10 inches off the one piece to length.

3

STEP 2: SAND THE SIDE PIECES.

Use an orbital sander or sandpaper to smooth the rough edges of the angled side pieces.

STEP 3: ATTACH THE ANGLED SIDE PIECES.

Place the two angled side pieces inside the edges of the third back piece and fasten in place from the back. There is no front piece for the third level of this assembly because of the angle of the final project.

Add an extra screw on each side toward the front to secure the side pieces in place because they will not attach to the corner braces.

STEP 4: INSTALL THE CORNER BRACES.

From one of the remaining cedar boards, cut two pieces that are 2½ × 16½ inches and two pieces that are 2½ × 11 inches. The long pieces are the braces for the back corners. Cut the ends of these on a slight angle to accommodate the gentle slope of the tops of the angled side pieces, or you can cut a bit shorter and install them below the angle. The window should close without leaving a gap further down. From the inside, screw these four braces to the outside frame to secure it in place.

STEP 5: TRIM THE FRONT.

If there is a bit of wood from the two angled pieces overlapping the front, use a dozuki handsaw or the orbital sander to gently trim it away.

STEP 6: ATTACH THE HINGES.

The preexisting metal piece along the back of the old window would have prevented the screws for the hinges from going in, so two scrap pieces of wood were trimmed and used to create a new "back" to which the hinges could be attached. This also pushed the window forward a bit to make up for the extra centimeters that were added from the diagonal. Once these scraps are screwed in place, attach the two hinges to the window frame and the frame of the box.

~ PLANT IT! ~

Niki Jabbour, also known as *the* year-round vegetable gardener, has extensive veggie gardens—and raised beds—in her Halifax, Nova Scotia, garden. She harvests throughout the winter, even when her cold frames are covered in snow! "Most cold frames have low profiles, making them ideal for compact salad greens," she says. Here, Niki shares some cold-frame-loving crops:

Arugula With its incredibly quick growth and excellent cold tolerance, arugula is a perfect choice for a fall and winter harvesting. Direct-seed plant three to five weeks before your expected fall frost, and begin harvesting when the leaves are 2 to 3 inches in length.

Mache This plant is so cold hardy, it doesn't actually need a cold frame in my zone 5 garden. But with our frequent snows, the frames make winter harvesting a snap. Each plant forms a 2- to 4-inch-wide rosette with tender and mildly nutty leaves. Harvest them whole by slicing the plants at soil level.

Kale In the fall and winter garden, kale is king, but the plants can grow quite large—up to four feet—so mature kale is protected with mini hoop tunnels. Our cold frames host baby kale, which is seeded in late summer and enjoyed for months.

Carrots If you've never tasted a just-picked carrot in January, you haven't lived! Winter carrots are super sweet, and we grow a handful of varieties for cold-season harvesting. The best flavor comes from varieties such as Napoli and YaYa. They should be seeded about 8 to 10 weeks before the first fall frost.

Turnips Hakurei Japanese turnips are a gourmet treat and popular at farmers' markets, but they offer a double harvest—high-quality roots *and* tasty greens. Seed them four to six weeks before the expected fall frost.

Even in the wickedest weather in the dead of winter, Niki Jabbour can still head out to her garden, brush the snow off the cold frames, and pick fresh vegetables for her family's dinner. *Niki Jabbour*

OTHER USES FOR COLD FRAMES

Besides being used to grow fresh crops during the cold, winter months, a cold frame can also come in handy for other functions—if it's empty, of course. Here are a few:

Harden off seedlings. When it's time to bring the wee little plants that you've grown indoors from seed out into the garden, you need to allow them to adapt to the elements. You can't just set them out in the sun because the delicate baby plants are not used to the hot rays or wind. Usually this means bringing plants outside to a protected spot for a few hours at a time, and then bringing them in at night over the course of a few days. A cold frame provides a perfect protected spot for plants to get used to being outdoors.

Store nursery plants. It's tempting to purchase plants at the nursery before the ground is ready for them. You can temporarily store impulse purchases in your cold frame—being sure to vent it if it gets too hot—until you're ready to put them in the garden.

Grow perennial seeds and propagate cuttings. Protect new plants that you've grown from seed or propagated from woody cuttings in your cold frame over the winter. Give them a little extra protection by covering them lightly with dry leaves or evergreen branches.

Overwinter plants that go dormant. Some plants simply shut down over the winter. Provided they're not too big, these can be placed inside a cold frame to comfortably hibernate until spring.

Get a head start by planting hardy annuals. As you wait for the ground to thaw, your cold frame can become a mini greenhouse, allowing you to grow a variety of plants from seed.

Once you have a regular raised bed, you'll want to add the indispensable cold frame to your garden inventory.
Sean James

GREENHOUSE COVER FOR RAISED BED

Designed and written by Jamie Gilgen
Photography by Donna Griffith
Illustration by Len Churchill

Just as a cold frame helps to prolong the growing season—or get a head start on it—a greenhouse also adds more flexibility to your planting options. Jamie Gilgen, a professional cyclist—and a skilled woodworker and green thumb—created this version of a greenhouse to fit over one of the raised beds she built. Gilgen is often away competing in cycling competitions, so she needed something that would allow her to protect a bountiful harvest despite not being in the garden every day to be able to vent her greenhouse.

A clever contraption called an automatic opener features a gas-charged cylinder that expands as the temperature inside the greenhouse climbs, prompting the arm that's attached to immediately and automatically prop open the side of the greenhouse. Venting is important when temperatures fluctuate so that you don't inadvertently cook the vegetables that are growing within.

In the summer, the design allows Gilgen to simply remove the side flaps of the greenhouse altogether so that the plants can breathe and thrive in their spot in the garden without having to move them.

Gilgen has generously shared her plans here to recreate this greenhouse that fits over a raised bed. You can modify the measurements to make it fit yours.

This plan is for a greenhouse that measures 4 × 5 feet × 18 inches at the base of the roof. The total height is 42 inches.

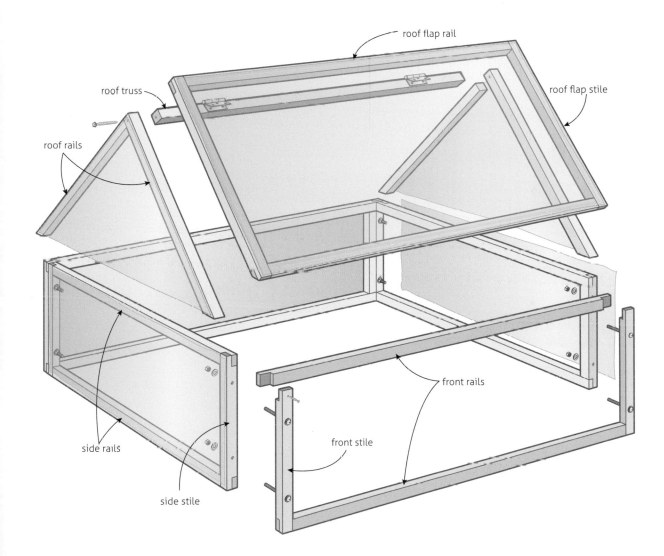

roof flap rail

roof truss

roof flap stile

roof rails

side rails

side stile

front rails

front stile

Tools

- A saw that can make cuts at a specific depth, such as a miter saw, table saw or circular saw
- Drill
- Drill bits
- Screwdriver
- Staple gun
- Eye and ear protection
- Work gloves

Materials

- Wood glue
- (14) 2 × 2" × 8'
- 3½" wood screws
- 1½" wood screws
- (2) Long wood screws with bolt ends
- Vapor barrier (6mil plastic film)
- (4) Hinges
- Stainless-steel staples

Bonus Options

- Heat-activated opener from Lee Valley
- Outdoor paint

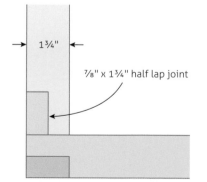

CORNER – TOP VIEW

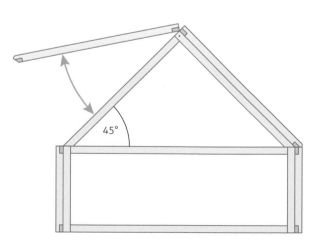

SIDE VIEW

HOW TO MAKE A
GREENHOUSE COVER
FOR RAISED BED

STEP 1: CREATE THE FRAME.

To create a rectangular frame that will act as the base of the greenhouse, you will need the following:

Cut two pieces of 2 × 2s to 5 feet long each, and cut two pieces of 2 × 2s 18 inches long each.

Lap joints are used in this project to join the lengths of wood together, which will result in a more rigid structure. Lap joints are the secret to being able to use 2 × 2s to build this structure and still have it be very sturdy. You could use butt joints, but the structure wouldn't be nearly as strong.

HOW TO MAKE A LAP JOINT To make lap joints, at the end of each of the four lengths that have just been cut, make a cut that is halfway through the wood and the same width as your lumber. If it's a 2 × 2, this is normally around 1¾ inches. If you have a tablesaw with a dado blade, this will be a very simple exercise; but if you don't, that's okay, it will just be a bit more manual. Once you have one cut that matches up with the width, create many more until you reach the end of the length. Then, use a chisel to remove the slivers of wood that are remaining. You will be doing this procedure a total of eight times, once for each end of wood.

Once you've completed the cuts, dry-assemble your pieces and make sure all the joints line up properly. Make any adjustments necessary. Drill pilot holes through each joint; these will be used to screw the joints together for even more strength.

After all of your pieces have been drilled, spread some glue on each surface of the joints. Make sure everything is aligned, and use a 1½-inch screw to join them together.

Once all of this is done, you will have completed one side of the greenhouse. Repeat this procedure and you will have completed both sides of the greenhouse.

You're now half done with the rectangular frame of the greenhouse. Repeat all of the above steps, but cut lengths from 2 × 2 stock using the following equation: 4' - (2" × 1¾") = 44.5". This is the same equation used for the roof truss.

STEP 2: CREATE THE ROOF.

The roof is built at a 45-degree angle so that it sheds snow well. This is especially important if you'll be using this structure as a cold frame. The roof is very simple: It consists of two lengths of 2 × 2 cut at 45-degree angles on each end.

CUTS FOR THE ROOF Cut four lengths of wood. They should be cut to 35½ inches long. Use a miter saw to cut each end at a 45-degree angle, so that when the two pieces are assembled, they butt together making a 90-degree angle and each end lays flat and true against the frame.

For the main roof truss, use another 2 × 2, and cut it to 5 feet minus 2 × the actual width of your lumber. For example, truss length = (5' × 12") - 2 × 1.75" = 56½".

SECURING THE JOINTS Drill pilot holes slightly offset so that you can screw each end of the roof at the apex together. Also drill two pilot holes on each end that will attach to the frame. Glue up the pieces, and screw them together. There are no fancy joints in this part of the structure.

For the main roof truss, drill through the apex of the two roof beams into the end of the main truss. This should be a deep hole and larger because you'll be using a very large bolt to secure it.

STEP 3: CREATE THE ROOF FLAPS

You'll be creating two roof flaps so that you can access the greenhouse from both sides. If you only want one flap, that's fine although I recommend two because this greenhouse is 4 feet wide and that's a long way to reach with only one flap.

For each flap, cut two pieces of 2 × 2 to 5 feet long and two pieces of 2 × 2 to about 34 inches long. Use your freshly honed lap joint skills to join the top two joints of each flap; for the bottom one, there is a special step. If you do not have a tablesaw that can cut at 45-degree angles, see below. Cut one of the 5-foot lengths at a 45-degree angle all the way across. This is a tricky cut, so if you have someone to help you, it's much safer. Once this is done, you should be able to just drill a pilot hole through the ends of the roof flap and butt joint it together.

I DON'T HAVE A TABLESAW If you don't have a tablesaw, you can just join the flaps like you did the other four sides of the greenhouse. The flap just won't sit perfectly flat at the interface between the rectangular structure and the flap.

STEP 4: ASSEMBLE ALL YOUR PARTS.

You now have two long rectangles and two short rectangles with triangles on top. If you don't want to be able to disassemble the greenhouse, just screw it all together. If you do, drill large holes and bolt it together. Once you have your rectangular base assembled, bolt in the main roof truss using the two large pilot holes made earlier. Now attach the flaps using the hinges.

STEP 5: WRAP YOUR GREENHOUSE.

You now have a sizable structure, but it's not a greenhouse yet. Cut pieces of a 6mil vapor barrier larger than each of the main areas of the frame. Staple them in place and cut off any excess. Use stainless-steel staples, if you can find them. It keeps your greenhouse looking pristine and rust-free. The vapor barrier expands and shrinks a lot with temperature, so wrap it at around 50 °F to avoid ripping and flapping.

OPTION:
ADD AN AUTOMATIC OPENER.
If you don't want to have to worry about cooking your precious plants, you can install an automatic opener. Cut two pieces of wood, and screw them into the frame. If you used untreated wood, be sure to add some type of finish to the outside to protect it.

AN INTRODUCTION TO HUGELKULTUR

Hugelkultur is technically a type of raised bed gardening, but one that does not require drilling or cutting or construction of any kind. Simply put, it's a garden on a hill. This garden concept originated in Germany and Eastern Europe. The "hill" is basically an artfully arranged pile of yard waste, namely fallen branches, sticks, and twigs mixed with soil and compost to create a rich and fertile ecosystem. These days, those who follow principles of permaculture in their garden are often the ones making hugel beds.

If you've ever heard of a nurse log in a forest, it's the same type of concept, except a hugelbed is manmade rather than a natural occurrence. A nurse log is born when a fallen tree starts to decay and naturally grows a garden—albeit a very wild one—atop the fallen log. On it you'll find plants like mosses, wildflowers, ferns, you name it. Whatever seeds blow in on the wind and decide that this log will make a good home will end up growing on a nurse log. And the wood underneath nourishes the plants as it decomposes.

To create your own hugel bed, there is a little more effort involved, though it's not terribly labor-intensive.

Allocate a space in your yard for your hugel bed (make sure it gets plenty of sunshine). Some gardeners prefer to dig a trench so that everything happens underground, but the most common way to build it is to clear a space and build up.

Add a layer of logs, branches, and twigs (making sure the largest lie on the bottom) that you've collected to form the base of the bed. Once everything is in place, this area will store rainwater and distribute it throughout the garden accordingly. Next, fill the gaps with leaves and straw, and then yard waste, like grass clippings and green leaves (be sure to avoid using anything that's visibly diseased). Lastly, add a layer of soil and compost.

Allow your new bed to sit for a few weeks before planting in it. In fact, you might want to create your bed in the fall and wait to plant until springtime. This gives the bed lots of time to settle in place.

As the wood breaks down over time, it will heat up, helping the roots of your plants grow and supplying the bed with valuable nutrients.

Note: You can use most kinds of wood, but be mindful of the ones that may inhibit the natural function of what a hugel bed is supposed to do. Avoid any material that will not decompose, such as redwood and black locust, and toxic trees including black walnut, which contain a toxin called "juglone."

AN INTRODUCTION TO KEYHOLE GARDENING

A keyhole garden is a type of raised bed, but its function extends beyond that of a typical raised bed. Keyhole gardens are generally round in shape. In the center of these beds you won't find plants. That's because the middle is reserved for a compost tower or "basket," as they're called—or, basically, a built-in fertilizer receptacle. You don't need to feed the soil in a keyhole garden throughout the growing season because it is already receiving nutrients from the compost being generated in the middle of the bed.

A slice of the keyhole garden is generally carved out to make a path to this central compost system. That's where the garden gets its name. If you were to get a good aerial view, you would see that the garden is actually shaped somewhat like a keyhole.

The concept for keyhole gardens stems from charitable organizations that were looking to find solutions for impoverished countries to successfully grow crops where the growing conditions can be extra challenging and severe. A keyhole garden creates an environment that retains moisture and is more nourishing and hospitable to edibles. It's also economical to put together because it focuses on materials that can be reused and recycled (though you can now buy kits that allow you to quickly and easily build your own keyhole garden).

A keyhole garden is usually about 6 feet across, which allows the gardener to easily access the plants from all sides. The garden's structure can be constructed using anything from cement blocks to old bricks or rocks. The bottom of the bed is lined with natural finds, including rocks, branches and twigs, or reusable items such as old bricks, plastic pots, and so on. These provide good drainage. Even tin cans may be placed here to provide a bit of iron for the soil as they rust. The planting space between this bottom layer and the top is comprised of layers of soil and compost as well as materials that are biodegradable, like cardboard and newspaper. The top layer of soil should slope away from the compost basket.

The compost bin in the center is typically made from a strong material such as hardware cloth or chicken wire that forms a circle shape about a foot to a foot-and-a-half wide from the bottom of the bed to just above the surface. This is where yard refuse like grass and leaves (avoid adding anything diseased) and kitchen waste is discarded, so it can break down and create the compost. Not only does this basket feed the soil, the compost itself warms it up.

Why would you want a keyhole garden in your yard? Well, if space is limited and you have to choose between a raised bed or a compost pile, a keyhole garden solves the dilemma. A keyhole garden is also very self-sustaining and lower maintenance for busy green thumbs.

TIPS FROM A KEYHOLE GARDEN TRIAL

On her blog, *More Than Oregano*, Beth Billstrom has written about her experience gardening in a keyhole garden made from a kit. While it's square-shaped, the bed still follows the basic principles of keyhole gardening by providing a basket in which you can add compost to feed your garden (and a path that allows for easy access to it).

Billstrom says that her keyhole garden is one of the healthiest gardens she's ever grown. "The layering of green materials and compost/soil gave the garden a healthy balance from the beginning," she says.

Here are a few of Billstrom's keyhole garden discoveries.

You can grow more in a small space with less effort. Beth Billstrom was dubious about planting all her edibles so close together, but she managed to squeeze 10 tomatoes, 8 pepper plants, and 10 basil plants into her 6 × 6" garden. She says she would have needed double the space in a traditional garden. *Beth Billstrom*

ABOVE: Kitchen waste is diverted from the landfill. Beth Billstrom was initially concerned with the size of the basket for the bed, but she soon realized it was easy to fill. She throws fruit and veggie scraps as well as non-diseased scraps from around the garden into the compost basket. She also used the lasagna method to build the soil in the actual garden before she planted. *Beth Billstrom*

RIGHT: Keyhole gardens prevent issues with four-legged pests. At 24 inches tall, Beth Billstrom's keyhole garden keeps rabbits, dogs, and neighborhood cats away. *Beth Billstrom*

WHAT IS PERMACULTURE?

Permaculture is a method of gardening that ties in all the various elements in nature—plants, insects, growing conditions—in a way where they can work together without intervention as a self-sufficient whole.

PROTECTED STRAWBERRY PLANTER

Designed and written by Chris Peterson
Photography by Tracy Walsh
Illustration by Bill Kersey

Strawberries are one of those first fruits of spring and summer that you'll find at the farmers' market. And there's something about heading to a local pick-your-own farm that really jump-starts a harvest season full of fresh preserves, healthy salads, and produce-packed smoothies. It's likely that the abundance of these delectable fruits available during strawberry season is due to the fact that the plants are so easy for farmers to grow.

Did you know that you could set up your own pick-your-own farm right in your backyard? Just be warned: unfortunately, animals and birds enjoy these sweet treats too.

Enter this 69-inch-wide octagonal raised bed. Voracious spreaders such as mint and chamomile get a bad rap, but strawberries are also pretty good at spreading out. Not only does this ingenious bed contain the plants, a handy lid lined with bird netting allows you to keep the fruit all to yourself—without having to share it with a neighborhood menagerie.

According to project designer Chris Peterson, building the planter frame can easily be done with a power miter saw. But you can also use a circular saw or a handsaw and a tall miter box. To increase or decrease the size of this raised bed, you can cut shorter or longer pieces. And, if you wish to change the shape of the planter, double the number of sides and divide that number into 360. (For example, a hexagon has six sides; therefore: 360 ÷ 12 = 30. Make each end cut at 30 degrees, and you'll have a perfect hexagon.)

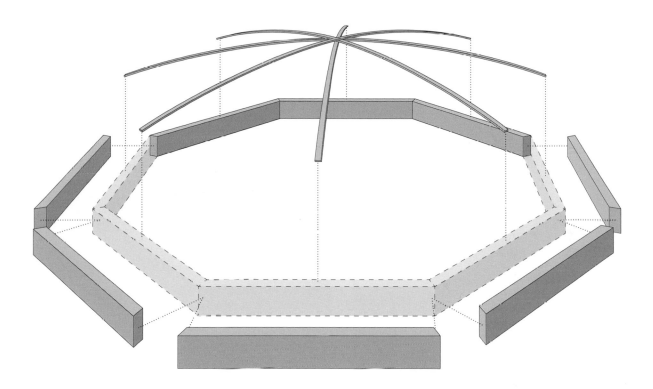

Tools

- Miter saw
- Cordless drill and bits
- Speed square
- Eye and ear protection
- Work gloves

Materials

- Waterproof wood glue
- 3" deck screws
- Bird netting
- (4) 2 × 4" × 8' boards
- (24') screen molding

Cut list

PART	DIMENSION	PCS
Planter side	$1\frac{1}{2} \times 3\frac{1}{2} \times 28\frac{1}{2}$"	8
Cover support	$\frac{1}{4} \times \frac{3}{4} \times 72$"	4

HOW TO MAKE A
PROTECTED STRAWBERRY PLANTER

1

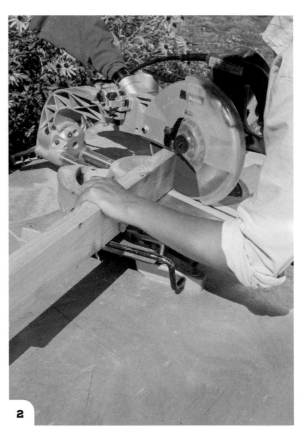

2

STEP 1: SET UP YOUR MITER SAW.

Run some test cuts to make sure the angle setting is accurate. Cut two pieces of scrap 2 × 4 at 22½ degrees. Fit the pieces together end to end, and check the assembly with a straight edge; the pieces should be perfectly straight. (If you're using a circular saw, cut test pieces with the saw blade tilted at 22½ degrees.)

STEP 2: CUT ALL SIDES TO THE SAME LENGTH.

Use a stop block setup to ensure that all pieces are precisely the same length. This speeds your work and ensures the joints will fit tightly. For this roughly 6-foot-wide planter, each piece is 28½ inches long, measuring between the long points of the two angled ends. To make the cuts, leave the miter saw set on one side and just flip the board over for each successive cut.

STEP 3: DRILL PILOT HOLES.

Drill pilot holes through one frame piece and into its mating piece, starting the hole about $\frac{7}{8}$ inch from the pointed end of the first piece. Angle the hole slightly toward the inside of the joint (what will be the inside of the assembled frame). This gives the screws a little bit of cross-grain penetration, helping them hold better than if they were perfectly parallel to the grain of the mating piece.

STEP 4: ASSEMBLE YOUR OCTAGONAL SHAPE.

Apply glue and fasten each joint with two screws. For extra strength, add a third screw driven from the opposite direction as the first two.

Tip: Work on a flat surface, such as a garage floor, to help keep the pieces flush at the top and bottom so the entire assembly will be flat.

STEP 5: PREPARE YOUR PLANTING SITE.
Dig out the grass and soil at least several inches deep and replace it with high-quality garden soil mix. Cover the soil with landscape fabric to keep unwanted grass or weeds from growing. Use nails or spikes to hold the fabric in place; then trim it flush with the octagon edges.

STEP 6: MAKE THE DOMED LID.
Create an arched dome with wooden screen molding (¼ × ¾ × 72-inch strips of wood). Predrill holes at each end for screws, using a drill bit bigger than the size of the screw. Mark the centers of each 2 × 4. Screw one end in, leaving the screw about ½ inch out of the wood. Move to the opposite side, arch the wood, and put a screw in on that side, tightening it just enough to hold the end down. Join the frame rails to the stiles with a metal corner at each stile.

STEP 7: PLANT YOUR STRAWBERRIES.
Spread an inch or two of mulch over the landscape fabric, then plant the octagon with your strawberry plants. Cut slits in the fabric where each plant goes, and then work the plant down into the garden soil.

8

STEP 8: ADD THE PROTECTIVE NETTING.
Spread bird netting over the dome. Hold it in place by hooking it on two roundhead screws or small nails on each side. Trim the excess. To take the netting off, wrap one side around a piece of smooth wood or a 6-foot-long pole and just roll it up. When you want to cover the strawberries in the spring, just hook one side and roll it out again.

A FEW PLANTING TIPS

Fill your new geometric raised bed with loamy soil that contains lots of organic matter. Strawberries don't take well to soil that has previously hosted sod and members of the nightshade family.

When planting young seedlings, make sure that the roots have a very light covering of soil and that the crown is exposed.

There are different types of strawberries, but everbearing varieties will provide more than one harvest between spring and fall.

RAISED BEDS DESIGNED FOR PRACTICAL PURPOSES

Besides being a very suitable home for growing edibles, raised beds can also be used for more practical purposes. For example, they can be used to grow plants that serve as privacy screens or as a useful physical barrier.

That's the function that the two raised beds shown here serve. Designed by landscape designer Shawn Gallaugher, these two planters sit on decks.

RAISED BED WITH A WATER FEATURE

The raised bed below was designed to include a privacy screen that shields views of the neighboring property. The arbor detail was added to offer a bit of shade. Gallaugher divided the raised bed into two sections: one for plants and the other for a soothing and decorative water feature.

To create the pond, the one half of the raised bed was lined with pond liner and fitted with an overflow pipe as well as a drain in the bottom. A Styrofoam cutout was strategically placed to hold the water pump. Then, the liner was covered with black pebbles to conceal the covered pump and the bottom.

Electricity to the pump runs under the deck. It also powers a light fixture in the pond that comes on at night. Six inches of wood coping was attached along the top of the planter so that people can sit on the edge of the water feature. A stainless-steel spout was attached to the trellis that's part of the arbor to give off some ambient noise.

The other half of the raised bed holds plants and decorative elements. The soil extends to the ground below the deck, allowing the roots and water to reach the ground.

RAISED BED FEATURING A CLOTHESLINE

The raised bed on the top of the opposite page sits in place of a railing along the edge of the deck. Gallaugher says it appears to be sunken and was meant to bring greenery to the floor level, so that the deck is not removed from the ground plantings. In fact, there are stepping stones so that the eco-friendly client, who got rid of the clothes dryer, can walk across them to hang clothing on the clothesline that's incorporated into the arbor. Outdoor drapes can also be added for additional privacy as well as for impromptu movie nights on the deck.

While the deck is not high enough to require a railing by code, the raised bed was built to provide an edge to the 20-inch drop off the deck and to make the deck safe. The arbor was also added to this raised bed to provide privacy and shade. It shields the deck from the balcony of a neighbor.

Gallaugher didn't add a bottom to this raised bed, so the roots of the plants can potentially grow into the ground.

Photos by Shawn Gallaugher

CHAPTER 6

NOT HANDY?
NO PROBLEM!

If you don't consider yourself particularly handy, fear not. There are so many raised bed options, from upcycling items such as old drawers and fruit crates, to using newfangled containers like fabric pots and plastic bins, to assembling easy-to-follow kits.

Raid your (or someone else's) shed, attic, basement, or property for items that you can repurpose into a raised bed—old washtubs, dresser drawers, bathtubs, wine crates, you name it! And remember: raised beds can be big or small. Even a deep container, such as a bucket or a rectangular recycling bin that was originally meant for newspapers, can yield a few veggies that grow below the soil, such as radishes, carrots, and beets, or house sun-lovers that need space for their roots, such as peppers or tomatoes. Your harvest may not produce enough to give away to neighbors, but it just might be enough to feed your family a few fresh homegrown meals.

If you have the space, but woodworking isn't one of your strengths, you can still have a standard wooden raised bed—no carpentry work required. Specially made steel or powder-coated aluminum corners allow for a relatively easy raised bed setup—all you need to do is drop in the wood, level it all out, and fasten everything together. For this task, a simple screwdriver may suffice. Or you may have to borrow a power drill from a neighbor if it's not in your arsenal of tools.

A few clever green thumbs have started companies that sell kits, meaning everything is cut to size, boxed up with all the hardware—and a set of directions—and delivered to your door. Some businesses will even build the raised beds for you.

But part of the fun is that sense of accomplishment when you've built something yourself—even if there was a minimum of handiwork required. The opportunities really are endless. Some take a little creativity but fewer tools than a woodworking project, while others can simply be set up in minutes and all you have to do is add soil—and the plants!

Stock tanks are especially useful as raised beds because they're basically ready to go. However, they do have a bottom. If there is a plug, you have a bit of an allowance for drainage, but if there isn't one at all, you have to make your own holes. The company that makes this corrugated-steel raised bed has eliminated the bottom altogether. The shell simply sits on the ground over the earth or pavement or stones—wherever you choose to place it. *Conquest Steel*

These raised beds, created using powder-coated aluminum corners from Gardener's Supply Company, prove that gardens can be made in all shapes and sizes to suit your space and needs—and you don't need woodworking skills to create them! *Gardener's Supply Company*

Not only can these Envirolok bags be used to create raised garden beds, the bags themselves can become a garden. A double-duty element to their utility is the fact that they can be used on a slope or to prevent erosion. *Sean James*

As mentioned in Why Garden in Fabric Pots? (see page 245), fabric gardens, which can simply be unfolded and filled with soil, can provide a healthy harvest of edibles. The company who makes the ones shown here, Woolly Pocket, also sells vertical gardening systems and has put together a kit for schools of living wall planters made from recycled milk jugs. *Kate Romero*

This raised bed takes the theme of "reduce, reuse, recycle" to a whole new level. And it proves that plants will pretty much grow anywhere in anything, provided their growing requirements are met. *Jessica Walliser*

The owner of this backyard replaced the grass with stone, concrete, and gravel to transform his space into a relaxing, low-maintenance oasis. Three galvanized steel raised beds were put together and filled with herbs and perennials. *Property of Tonic Magazine Inc./Landscape Design by Jamie Bussin/Photos by Michele Crockett*

Many stock tanks are oval in shape, but you can also find round ones, which make for an interesting addition to the yard. *Niki Jabbour*

These raised beds show off another example of the types of corners available for purchase. Although they're more utilitarian in design and aesthetic, they simplify the process of building raised beds and create orderly, contained rows of gardens. *Lorraine Flanigan*

This is another example of how you can grow a successful potato crop without having a traditional garden. Simply create a circular shape with a piece of fencing or similar material. Use cable ties to secure the ends. Line your new raised bed with newspaper, and fill the bottom with a bit of soil. Plant your spuds, and as the plants start to grow, continue to add newspaper along the sides and cover the stalks with more soil to about one-third from the top of the plant. *Jessica Walliser*

Utilitarian corners hold boards firmly in place and don't take any woodworking know how to install.

Exceptionally big cement slabs provide the perfect outline for a grouping of raised beds. *Jessica Walliser*

A stock tank garden doesn't just have to be a home for edibles. It can cleverly be used as a living privacy screen on a deck or patio. This one has been planted with evergreen shrubs along the back and annuals such as sweet potato vine and coleus along the front. The garden has been placed on a dolly so that it can be moved around easily throughout the garden. *Proven Winners*

An old seed drill has been reconfigured as a raised bed to hold colorful ornamental annuals. *Tara Nolan*

TURN A STOCK TANK INTO A GARDEN

Designed by Jon Carolftis
Photography by Proven Winners

Stock tanks were invented to provide water for thirsty livestock, but these days, creative green thumbs are reimagining them as gardens for edibles, ornamentals—even for bog plants. They're the perfect ready-to-go raised bed. It's pretty easy to convert a stock tank into a garden. Even if you don't consider yourself particularly handy, all you need to do is add a few holes to the bottom for drainage—and take out the plug if one exists (simply cover the hole with landscape fabric to keep the soil inside).

To make it even easier, many companies are now creating stock tank frames specifically for gardeners that mimic the look of a traditional stock tank but without the metal bottom. This stock tank can simply be placed anywhere you like—in the garden, on interlocking brick, on a cement patio, and so on.

Metal washbasins also will do the trick. These are easily found in hardware stores or anywhere that sells livestock supplies. Antique markets may also reveal a variety of old, sturdy washbasins in a range of shapes and sizes.

If you're searching for a stock tank online, use the keywords "stock tank" or "utility tub."

Real stock tanks typically have a plug in the bottom. This should be removed when you're turning your new stock tank into a garden so the water can drain out.

If you like the galvanized metal look, you can leave it. But a stock tank can also be painted.

Add holes to your stock tank with a high-speed steel (HSS) drill bit, which is meant for cutting metal. Adding a bit of oil to the bit while you drill will keep it cool and speed up the cutting.

At the Toronto Botanical Garden, bottomless stock tanks made by a local steel company have been used to grow everything from tomatoes, peppers, and okra to leafy greens. These raised beds show urban green thumbs who visit the public garden that they don't need a ton of space to grow a successful veggie crop. "It is so important for gardeners of all ages to realize that they are able to grow fresh, organic veggies even in the absence of a traditional in-ground garden," says Paul Zammit, the Nancy Eaton director of horticulture at the Toronto Botanical Garden. "Raised beds are the solution. The harvest tastes great and the experience is incredible."
Tara Nolan

FALSE-BOTTOM FAKERY

One of Paul Zammit's tricks to avoid breaking the bank when purchasing soil to fill his stock tanks is to create false bottoms, so you only have to fill part of the container. (This can also be done to keep the overall weight of the stock tank down.) According to Zammit, the Nancy Eaton Director of Horticulture at the Toronto Botanical Garden, it's all about layering!

Step 1: Turn over a few empty plastic pots and place at the bottom of the container.

Step 2: Cover the plastic pots with slabs of old, rot-resistant, untreated wood.

Step 3: Line the stock tank with landscape fabric.

Step 4: Use binder clips or clamps to hold the landscape fabric in place while you fill the stock tank with soil.

Photos by Tara Nolan

Step 5: Add soil, remove the binder clips, and tuck any visible pieces of the landscape fabric under the soil so you can't see it. *Paul Zammit*

Niki Jabbour

The tomatoes in this stock tank are clearly thriving in their raised bed home. *Conquest Steel*

Tara Nolan

MAKE A RAISED BED USING CORNERS

Photography by Donna Griffith
Corners provided by Gardener's Supply Company

Want to learn about a fabulous invention that will allow you to have a raised bed in your yard with minimum effort? Raised bed corners. All you need to do is pick up a few lengths of wood from your local lumberyard or home center (or have it delivered). Not too much else is required for this project.

Corners allow you to have a wooden raised bed without the construction work. There are several different types of corners you can purchase from a variety of retailers. Some have a more utilitarian look while others are modern and stylish—perfect if you're putting them in a front or side yard where they will be seen.

Using corners to make a raised bed gives you a few customization options because you control the lengths of wood that are used. So if you have a long, narrow yard with a thin strip of sun, for example, you could create a long, narrow raised bed. Midpoint pieces keep long projects stable. There are also a variety of different heights, giving you a choice of timber size.

You can even find interesting connectors, which allow you to get creative with the shape of your raised bed. In other words, think outside the box and make a triangle or a star!

The corners shown here are from Gardener's Supply Company, an online retailer that offers several corner options. These are made from a powder-coated aluminum. We used them to make a 3 × 6 bed.

Tools

- Power drill or impact driver with a Phillips drill bit
- Level
- Tape measure
- Eye and ear protection
- Work gloves

Materials

- (2 sets) 10" corners
- (3) 2" × 10" × 6' cedar boards

Cut list

PART	DIMENSION	PCS
Short side	2" × 10" × 3'	2
Long side	2" × 10" × 6'	2

STEP 1: PUT THE CORNERS INTO POSITION.

Prepare the area where you want your raised bed to live and remove any grass, if necessary.

Place the corners roughly where you want them to go and insert the boards into the slots.

STEP 2: ATTACH THE CORNERS TO THE WOOD.

Once you're happy with where everything is placed, use a drill or impact driver to secure the wood to each corner with the screws provided. Add the end caps to the tops of the corners.

STEP 3: PREPARE THE BED FOR PLANTING.

Check the bed for level and amend the area accordingly.

PLANT IT!

Be aware of where the light is in the garden, and place the plants you think will be the tallest in a spot where they won't throw shadows on the rest of your crops that also need the sun.

WHY GARDEN IN FABRIC POTS?

Fabric pots have been available for a while in the commercial gardening industry, but they're fairly new to the consumer market. They're lightweight and usually made out of geotextiles; that is, fabric that's porous, allowing the soil to conserve water and drain easily. This same permeability also aerates the soil and roots, which is beneficial to the plants—it prevents them from becoming rootbound, instead allowing the plants to grow strong, healthy roots. This is a bonus on rooftops or pavement, which can become very hot in the sunshine. Certain containers can end up cooking your delicate plant roots and microorganisms if they're overheated.

Fabric pots come in many different shapes and sizes. Some are around the size of the raised beds for yards that are outlined in this book. Others are more compact and perfect for smaller spaces, like balconies or a wee corner where you want to grow some produce. Fabric pots are especially useful for rooftop gardens where weight can be an issue. Some designs have handles, allowing them to be easily moved around.

TOP LEFT: Fabric pots can pack in a multitude of plants, just like their plastic or wooden cousins. *Niki Jabbour*

TOP RIGHT: Even trellises can be added to fabric raised beds to support vining crops like beans. *Tara Nolan*

BOTTOM LEFT: This willow arch, a tangle of whip-thin saplings that are rooted in four fabric pots and woven to create a leafy dome, is the perfect shady place to read a book on a hot summer afternoon. *Tara Nolan*

BOTTOM RIGHT: This herb planter can be placed almost anywhere, so a home cook can have herbs close at hand. *Tara Nolan*

Some fabric pots, depending on what's planted in them, could easily be moved into a shed or garage to overwinter and then pulled back out in the spring. Just be sure to replenish the soil with compost or organic potting soil to add in some nutrients. Others can be emptied of their soil and plants, folded up, and stored pretty much anywhere—just be sure they're completely dry before you put them away.

You can plant everything from tomatoes to root vegetables in fabric pots, depending on their size.

Another bonus of using a fabric pot? It's *great* for containing voracious spreaders that you wouldn't normally want to plant right in your garden—like mint or chamomile. In fact, these pots should be mandatory for growing plants that spread. *Sean James*

BURLAP-WRAPPED PLASTIC PAILS

Designed by Tara Nolan
Photography by Donna Griffith

It's not uncommon to see those white plastic utility pails one might use to mix paint lining a driveway or alleyway, bursting with tomatoes and other veggies. Often, the green thumb who planted them is taking advantage of the optimal growing conditions offered by that particular spot. Even though a tall bucket full of plants would technically fall under container gardening, it's also a type of raised bed—albeit one that is more compact. These raised beds are also relatively easy to move from one sunny spot to another—or to somewhere to hibernate for the winter. (A wheelbarrow or garden cart is advised if you're lugging them somewhere full of soil.)

This project is very accessible to any level of DIY skill because it merely involves using sturdy burlap to tidy up those pails that might be sporting logos, or have signs of wear and tear. The burlap for this project came in the form of coffee bean bags, which were the perfect size to double up and wrap around the buckets. You can also purchase burlap at some garden centers and at fabric stores, and some offer burlap in decorative prints.

Tools

- Drill with a ⅜" drill bit
- Scissors
- Eye and ear protection

Materials

- Burlap (coffee bean bags or purchased in rolls)
- Needle and thread
- Large safety pins (optional)
- Colorful twine (optional)

STEP 1: PREPARE THE BUCKET FOR THE BURLAP.

Drill a few holes into the bottom of your bucket. Add a thin layer of gravel for drainage, or simply fill the bucket with good-quality potting soil that's meant for edibles.

STEP 2: WRAP THE BUCKET.

The burlap used for the pails shown here was already sewn into a bag that held coffee beans, meaning it was of double thickness and there was a folded seam at the bottom. Wrap the burlap around the outside of the bucket, using pins to hold it in place. The burlap should come right to the ground at the bottom of the bucket, and there should be some excess material to fold over the top to the inside, where it will be covered when you add the potting soil.

STEP 3: SECURE WITH A STITCH OR SAFETY PINS.

Use a simple whipstitch to sew the burlap around the bucket. Or secure the burlap in place with safety pins (keep in mind they may rust when left outside over the summer). Alternatively, you can tie some fancy rope or twine around the bucket to add a finishing touch.

PLANT IT!

Add no more than one plant to each pail. For edibles such as tomatoes and peppers, which later in the season may droop under the weight of their fruit, add some type of plant support, like a small tomato cage, while the plants are still young (if you wait to add the support later, you may break the plants). A stake, such as a sturdy bamboo stick, allows you to hold the plant up with garden twine if it starts to pitch forward due to its weight.

Tomatoes grow well in five-gallon pails because there's lots of space for their roots. *Tara Nolan*

RAISED BED IDEAS

REPURPOSING
OLD OBJECTS AS RAISED BEDS

Use your imagination to turn something that's lying around the house or hiding out in a garage or behind a shed into a ready-made raised bed garden. Everything from wine crates and whiskey barrels to washbasins and bathtubs can be fashioned into a garden. Just be mindful of the materials from which they're made because you don't want any harmful substances leaching into your healthy soil.

MAKE A BARREL BED

Many old barrels that were once used to hold whiskey or a fine wine are sold by the half. Talk about a ready-to-go raised bed! All you need to do is add some holes to the bottom for drainage.

LINE A BED WITH NATURAL MATERIALS—
NO ASSEMBLY REQUIRED!

If you're completely construction-challenged, you can use logs and tree stumps to create a natural, raised border around a bed. This one was plunked right on top of a sandy area. Good-quality soil was added in the center, which enabled flowers, trees, and edibles to be planted and thrive, despite the poor conditions surrounding them.

RECYCLE A RECYCLING BIN

Why do recycling bins make perfect raised beds? Well, they're a great height for a variety of different edibles, from root crops that grow under the soil to climbers like beans and bushier plants like tomatoes. Some already have drainage holes, and if they don't, it's easy to quickly add some. Over the winter, the bins can be emptied and cleaned, and then stacked (make sure they're dry) and stored.

ABOVE: Want to make a raised bed on a budget? Use tree trunks as your raised bed sides.

BELOW: This barrel holds an assortment of herbs that are regularly snipped throughout the season. Some, like the chives, are perennial and come back each spring. Other herbs, like the parsley, are replanted every year. The parsley also attracts swallowtail butterfly caterpillars, who munch on its tasty foliage before they create their chrysalis. *Donna Griffith*

Plant Potatoes in a Recycling Bin

Many don't think of potatoes when they're choosing what to plant in their edible garden. But potatoes are quite easy to grow, and you don't need an actual garden in which to plant them. Deep containers can be used as mini raised beds for a bountiful crop of fries-to-be.

To plant, place a few inches of soil mixed with compost in the bottom of the container. Place the potatoes evenly on the soil so they're not touching. Cover with about 6 inches of soil mixed with more compost, and lightly water. Once the plants start to grow, wait until they reach about 6 to 8 inches and then cover up to three-quarters of the stem and surrounding foliage with soil. Keep doing this throughout the season until the plants stop growing.

Make a Wire Frame to Grow Potatoes

Another way to grow potatoes is to create a wire-framed, cylindrical raised bed out of fencing or chicken wire. Use zip ties or some type of clip to hold the seam closed. Line the sides with newspaper, add a few inches of soil, and plant your seed potatoes. Then cover with about 3 inches of soil. When the plants reach about 9 inches tall, add a bit more newspaper around the edges, and mound the soil around two-thirds of the plant. Keep repeating this step until you've reached the top of your raised bed.

TOP: It's unlikely you'll find potato plants at a nursery. Instead, you need to be on the lookout for what are referred to as "seed potatoes." These are generally available in late spring in paper bags. *Paul Zammit*

MIDDLE: For small containers, look for smaller potato varieties, such as French fingerling or banana. Bigger spuds can go into your large raised beds. *Paul Zammit*

BOTTOM: Make sure each piece of potato has an eye—this is where the plants will start to grow. *Paul Zammit*

CHAPTER 7

SUPPORT YOUR PLANTS

———

Once your raised beds are happily situated in the garden—or in your front yard, on the balcony, back deck, or rooftop—the next step is choosing what delicious edibles you're going to plant. Despite spacing out your plants correctly, once they take off, they may start to encroach on their neighbors. Some plants, like zucchinis, cucumbers, pumpkins, and melons, grow outward on vines, wrapping their tendrils around anything they encounter. Other plants, such as tomatoes and peppers, start to grow tall but can send branches out in other directions. And then you have climbers, such as peas, cucumbers, and beans that like to work their way up toward the sky.

All of these plants can use a little help and would be happy with a trellis that they can climb. The heat-seekers such as tomatoes will benefit from some staking or caging well before they start to grow too big and lean over from the weight of their fruit. Those eager climbers will be happy winding their way around an obelisk, ladder, or other such garden support. And if you help your plants grow up, you'll save space in the garden and maintain some order between the rows.

In this chapter, you'll find a collection of stakes, trellises, cages, and other helpful supports. There are suggestions that can be used in raised beds located in a yard as well as those confined to a small space.

Be inspired by an easy DIY tomato "condo"; marvel over a squash arch that curves over a couple of raised beds, creating a living entryway to the veggie patch; and make your own obelisk. Ready-to-use stakes and cages can be purchased at a garden center. And even a trio of bamboo poles and some twine can create an instant support for bush beans.

———

PLANT SUPPORT
INSPIRATION

This tomato trellis keeps the sprawling branches of indeterminate tomato plants in check. *Niki Jabbour*

Majestic obelisks in these gardens add character and refinement to any raised bed. *Tracey Ayton*

Upcycle items to use as plant supports: Old ladders make perfect plant trellises for climbers like squash, cucumbers, and melon. Just be sure to place a ladder deeply and firmly in the ground. You might even lean it toward a sturdy structure, like a fence.

A-frames made from sturdy material such as bamboo sticks form three rows on either side of this bed. Strips of plastic fencing run along the sides along with smaller vertical sticks that are tied in place with twine. *Niki Jabbour*

Build a squash arch: If you look closely past the vines, you'll see that there's a squash arch holding everything up. This is the brainchild of blogger Amy Andrychowicz. It's made from PVC piping and fencing, and can be used to train everything from pumpkins to butternut squash. The arch also keeps the fruit off the ground, which prevents them from being eaten by pests or rotting in the soil. You can find full DIY instructions to build the squash arch on Andrychowicz's blog, *Get Busy Gardening. Amy Andrychowicz*

Construct a tomato condo: Jamie Gilgen, who designed and built the greenhouse on page 216, put together these tomato condos, as she calls them, in the spring when her plants were still small. As you can see, the plants need them. They obviously love the growing conditions they're provided with and thrive in this sunny spot in the garden. *Donna Griffith*

Brace a bamboo tripod: Use garden twine to turn three sturdy bamboo poles into a tripod for climbers such as beans. Look for bamboo poles in home and garden centers and even discount stores. *Donna Griffith*

PLANT SUPPORT
INSPIRATION

Flowerpot power: Even a simple flowerpot turned upside down can be used to raise delicate branches up off the ground. This can be a big help for vining plants, like cucumbers. *Bren Haas*

Make an A-frame trellis over a pathway: Rather than cover valuable raised bed real estate, each side of this trellis, built by blogger Andrea Hungerford of *On Blueberry Hill*, is secured to the edge of a raised bed with the trellis leaning away from the garden and toward its parallel counterpart on the other side. Cattle fencing was placed between the frame supports to serve as a lattice that the vining veggies will climb. Once edibles such as peas start to climb this framework, they create a tunnel down the center of the garden.
Andrea Hungerford

A wider plant support provides ample room for vining plants to climb.

When left in place, metal hoops that hold a row cover find another occupation as plant supports, allowing climbing edibles to wrap their tendrils around them as they reach upward. *Meighan Makarchuk*

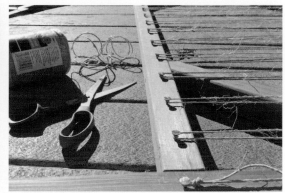

Trellises and twine: This trellis, created by Ian Wilson of Portland Edible Gardens, is a great DIY project that can be created with a few woodworking skills. *Ian Wilson*

1. This will be a sturdy frame that can be attached to the back of a raised bed. *Ian Wilson*

2. Evenly spaced nails are hammered to within a quarter to half an inch from the wood along the top and bottom of the frame. *Ian Wilson*

3. Then garden twine is tied and looped around vertically to complete this sturdy plant support. *Ian Wilson*

4. This trellis can be stored over the winter and restrung year after year. *Ian Wilson*

Simple A-frame structures made from sticks work as plant supports, proving that you might be able to look no further than your backyard to find the materials needed for supports.

Even before plants start their climb, obelisks project a feeling of English-garden sophistication. *Niki Jabbour*

This curved plant support gives peas lots of space to climb up and away from the other plants below.
Bren Haas

It's amazing how a few pieces of wood and some string will suffice when it comes to building a sturdy plant support.

Striking plant supports provide symmetry in this garden. *Donna Dawson*

Add a dash of color to the extreme green in your garden by painting your plant supports a vibrant hue. *Niki Jabbour*

A SIMPLE LASHING TECHNIQUE

If you have some sturdy sticks or pieces of bamboo out of which you'd like to make a quick and easy DIY trellis, use this lashing technique to hold it all together and make a strong, durable support system for your plants. All you need is a roll of garden twine. Waxed twine is a bit stickier than the regular version, so it may help things stay in place better.

1. Crisscross two pieces of bamboo where you'd like to join them together. Fold a 4-foot-long piece of twine in half, and wrap it around the bottom piece.

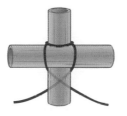

2. Pull both ends of the twine across the top cane, and cross them underneath the bottom cane.

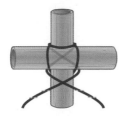

3. Pull the twine ends back up, and cross them over the top cane.

4. Cross the twine underneath the joint, forming an X.

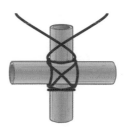

5. Lift the ends up, and make an X across the top of the joint.

6. Wrap the bottom cane from below and then across the top, next to the joint.

7. Wrap the bottom cane on the other side of the joint.

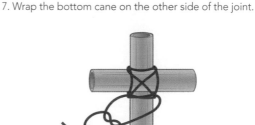

8. Tie a square knot and then trim off the twine ends.

**A CLASSIC
GARDEN OBELISK**

The obelisk shape—four long sides with a tapered, triangular top—appears in historical monuments dating back to ancient Egypt and Greece, and all the way throughout history to modern times.

In the garden, however, an obelisk sits proudly among the plants, providing support to a variety of crops year after year. A common design is four sturdy legs set into the soil that meet at the top to form a triangular shape. Often by the end of the season, the tapered top, perhaps capped with a fancy finial, is barely visible through the foliage of whatever plant it happens to be supporting. But until that stage, obelisks are lovely, not to mention invaluable, additions to the garden.

Because of their stately stature, obelisks have long been used as decorative elements in formal gardens. However, they're especially useful in gardens full of edibles where they can help maximize space and train trailing vines of certain plants to grow upward rather than outward. And, of course, obelisks can add a great deal of visual interest and sophistication to a simple, standard raised bed.

Obelisks can be made from a variety of materials, including wood, sticks, or wrought iron. They can be simple or ornate, welded, woven, or nailed together. The obelisk shown here requires a bit of woodworking expertise, but you only need three tools to build it: a saw, a drill, and a carpenter's square. And as for materials, use a rot-resistant wood of your choosing.

Tools

- Drill
- Drill bits including a countersink bit
- Saw (hand, jigsaw, or circular)
- Carpenter's square
- Clamps
- Eye and ear protection
- Work gloves

Materials

- (4) 2 × 2" × 8' boards
- (3) 1 × 2" × 8' boards
- Pine screen retainer molding
- (2) 10' molds
- (1) round finial
- (1 lb. each) 2" and 2½" deck screws
- (8) 4d galvanized finish nails

Cut list

PART	DIMENSION	PCS
Leg	1½ × 1½ × 61"	4
Lower crosspiece	¾ × 1½ × 22" *	4
Upper crosspiece	¾ × 1½ × 16" *	4

* Cut to size

HOW TO MAKE A
CLASSIC GARDEN OBELISK

STEP 1: MEASURE THE TOP OF EACH LEG.
Mark the tops of the four legs for trimming. Each leg top should be trimmed so that it has two beveled faces that meet in a point; then trim them to length. Using a carpenter's square, mark a wedge shape on two adjoining faces at the top. The wedge should be 1 inch wide at a point 5 inches down from the top of the leg. Then, using a straightedge, extend all four lines all the way to the edge of the workpiece. This will create two wedge shapes between 6 and 7 inches long. These wedges will be trimmed off in the next step.

STEP 2: TRIM AND FINISH THE TOPS.
Using a handsaw, cut off one of the wedges to create a wedge-shaped waste piece. Then flip your workpiece a quarter turn, and cut off the other wedge. This piece won't be a complete wedge like the other one since some of the wood has already been cut away. To finish trimming the leg tops, make a crosscut that follows the two 1-inch cutting lines that you drew. This will leave a top that is 1 × 1-inch and is angled, so it will be level when the legs are equally spread out in the garden.

Make the other tops the same way. When you're finished, the four legs should fit together to form a flat 2 × 2-inch top with the leg bottoms 24 inches apart.

STEP 3: MAKE THE LEG FRAMES.
Space an obelisk leg pair 24 inches apart from outside to outside at the bottom, and clamp or wedge them between two pieces of wood spaced to 24 inches apart. Clamp the beveled top ends together—the legs should naturally be close to 24 inches. Cut a 1 × 2 to 22 inches long, lay it across the legs 12 inches from the bottom, and then mark and cut the 1 × 2 flush with the legs. Fasten with 2-inch screws driven through pilot holes. Cut and fasten another crosspiece 16 inches above the lower crosspiece (center to center). Join the tops of the 2 × 2 legs with a 2½-inch screw. Drill pilot holes to make way for the , to avoid splitting the ends. Remove the assembled leg pair so that you can repeat this step for the other two obelisk legs.

STEP 4: ASSEMBLE THE OBELISK.
Stand the two assembled leg pairs upright with the tops joined together. Use a clamp to hold them together, and space the legs 24 inches apart. Mark two more sets of crosspieces, this time cutting them flush with the 1 × 2s. Fasten them to the 2 × 2s that are already installed, using screws driven through predrilled pilot holes. Screw the four tops together.

Note: If you want the 1 × 2s to match perfectly at the corners, make compound miter cuts on the ends. Trace the leg on a horizontal 1 × 2, then draw a 45-degree line from both the top and bottom of the line, connect them on the face of the 1 × 2, and cut that angle.

You can also add diagonal crosspieces on the sides to form an × pattern. Use screen retainer molding. Hold pieces of the molding in position, and mark cutting lines directly on the molding. Cut it to fit using a handsaw. Attach it in an × pattern with 4d galvanized finish nails.

Add the finial to the top. If you're using a standard finial from a home center, drill a hole for the integral lag screw in the center of the top, and thread it in. If your finial doesn't come with an integral lag screw, nail and glue the finial to the tops of the posts. Apply paint or stain to add polish to your project.

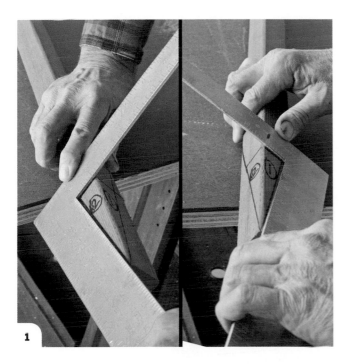

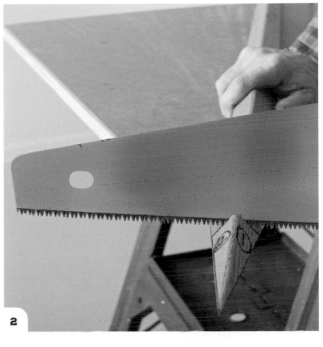

SANDWICH
BOARD TRELLIS

There's no getting around it. Certain plants are born climbers, and they aren't going to do as well when they're allowed to simply spread out along the ground in the garden. No matter what you use as a trellis, providing an environment for certain vining veggies to climb rather than spread not only lifts the fruit off the ground, it also maximizes your raised bed space. Now you have more room available in the garden to plant other edibles.

Plants like peas and cucamelons benefit from having a trellis on which they can grow up. If your structure is sturdy enough, you can also train heavier vining edibles, like melon, zucchini, and cucumbers to grow upward.

This project takes the design of a typical sidewalk sandwich board and turns it into a trusty trellis. Two identical frames are created and fastened together using hinges. It's easy to customize the dimensions of the frames to fit the raised bed where you'll be placing the finished trellis (stronger boards may also be used to support heavier plants). For this version, pointed feet have been added to keep the trellis itself up as well as off the ground, to prevent it from rotting. Furthermore, using heavy jute or hemp twine means you can compost everything at the end of the season instead of painstakingly unwinding the vines from the rope. Then, you can simply replace the trellis with fresh twine for the next crop.

If that empty space underneath the A-frame is bothering you after planting, you can put lettuces or spinach there; they'll benefit from a bit of the shade provided by the plants climbing the other side of the sandwich board. That way, you take advantage of every bit of raised bed real estate.

Tools

- Tape measure
- Circular saw
- Drill and drill bits
- Carpenter's square
- Scissors
- Marker
- Clamps
- Eye and ear protection
- Work gloves

Materials

- (6) 1 × 4" × 8' cedar
- (32) 1¼" deck screws
- (12) 2" deck screws
- (2) 3" galvanized or stainless-steel outdoor butt hinges with screws
- 250' heavy jute or hemp twine

Cut list

PART	DIMENSION	PCS
Frame stiles	¾ × 3½ × 72"	4
Frame rails	¾ × 3½ × 48"	4
Feet	¾ × 3½ × 12"	4

HOW TO MAKE A
SANDWICH BOARD TRELLIS

STEP 1: CUT THE FRAME PARTS.
Use a circular saw or power miter saw to cut your cedar to length. For this version, you will need four side pieces cut to 72 inches, and four top and bottom pieces cut to 48 inches.

STEP 2: TEST-FIT THE FRAME PIECES.
On a work table, line up two frame stiles and two frame rails so that the end pieces are on top of the side pieces and everything is flush. Check the corners with a carpenter's square and clamp in place.

STEP 3: ASSEMBLE THE FRAME.
With the parts all lined up, drill pilot holes through the side and end pieces. Fasten them together with four 1¼-inch deck screws. Repeat for all sides and assemble the other frame in the same way.

STEP 4: CUT THE FEET.
Using scraps of wood, cut four pieces to 12 inches each. To create the pointed ends, at one end of each foot piece, use a pencil to mark the center of the board's width (about 1¾ inches from the side edges). Then mark each side edge at 2 inches from the same end of the foot. Draw a line between the side marks and the center mark. Clamp your workpiece to the table securely, and cut along the lines using a circular saw (or a handsaw or jigsaw).

STEP 5: INSTALL THE FEET.

Place the top of the foot on the top edge of the bottom piece of the frame. Drill pilot holes; then use two or three 2-inch deck screws to fasten the foot in place. Be sure to make note where the original frame screws were so that you can offset these.

STEP 6: MARK YOUR HOLE LOCATIONS FOR THE TWINE.

Using a pencil and a tape measure, mark where the holes will go along the sides, top, and bottom edges of each frame. Mark 1 inch from the inside edge. Holes should be about 6½ inches apart in the exact same place on both frames. Make sure you drill holes that are slightly bigger than the thickness of your twine.

STEP 7: ATTACH THE HINGES.

With the tops of your two frames facing each other, place the butt hinges about 5 inches from the side of the top pieces so that each side of the hinge is touching one of the frames. Drill pilot holes, and then attach the hinges with the screws that came with them.

STEP 8: THREAD THE TWINE HORIZONTALLY.

Cut 22 pieces of twine, each about 60 inches long. Starting with the horizontal rows, feed the twine through the holes and knot it on the inside-facing part of the frame. Pull it across and knot it securely.

9

STEP 9: ADD THE VERTICAL TWINE PIECES.

Cut 14 pieces of twine, about 96 inches long. Guide your twine through the holes along the top of the frame, knotting each piece on the inside as you did for the sides. As you guide the vertical length of twine to each horizontal row, keep it taut and wrap it once around the horizontal piece; then move to the next. Try to keep an orderly grid as you go. Secure it through the corresponding hole at the bottom of the frame and tie it off on the inside. You can move the twine back and forth to neaten it out after you're finished securing all the pieces. Repeat this step for the other frame.

INSTEAD OF TWINE, YOU CAN ALSO USE . . .

Use chicken wire (also called poultry netting) or any wire with similar hole sizes in place of the twine. With work gloves on, use wire cutters to cut two pieces that are 46 × 70 inches. Then center one over each frame and, keeping it taut, use galvanized staples to secure it in place.

For edibles such as melons, squash, and other vining plants that produce heavy fruit, use vinyl-coated fencing as your web. Using the steps from the trellis project, take about 2 inches off the top, bottom, and side pieces so that you have a smaller frame. Cut a piece of fencing to fit, and secure it in place with galvanized staples, keeping it taut as you work.

RESOURCES AND CONTRIBUTORS

RAISED BED KITS, MATERIALS, PLANS, AND BUILDERS

Bonnie Plants designed the Tiered Planter on page 138 and the Raised Bed with Benches on page 106
www.bonnieplants.com

Conquest Steel donated the corrugated steel sheets for the Galvanized Planter on page 152
www.conqueststeel.com

Creative Living and Growing With Bren
www.brenhaas.com

Envirolok Vegetated Environmental Solutions
www.envirolok.com

Freedom Growing donated the purple Elevated Planter Box Kit on page 144
www.freedomgrowing.com

Gardener's Supply Company donated the corners for the Raised Bed with Corners project on page 242
www.gardeners.com

Lee Valley Tools
www.leevalley.com

Ohio State University Extension
www.ohioline.osu.edu

Portland Edible Gardens
www.portlandediblegardens.com

Rutgers Cooperative Extension
www.njaes.rutgers.edu

Seattle Urban Farm Company
www.seattleurbanfarmco.com

Smart Pot
In Canada: www.urbainculteurs.org
In the United States: www.smartpot.com

Backyard Urban Farm Company
www.bufco.ca

Urban Reclaimed Custom Furniture From Scott McKinnon
www.urbanreclaimed.wordpress.com

University of Maryland Extension
www.extension.umd.edu

Woolly Pocket
www.woollypocket.com

PLANTS AND SEEDS

Anything Grows Seed Company
www.anythinggrows.com

Baker Creek Heirloom Seeds
www.rareseeds.com

The Cottage Gardener
www.cottagegardener.com

Loblaws (donated gift cards to purchase many of the plants and soil for the raised beds)
www.loblaws.ca

Matchbox Garden & Seed Co.
www.matchboxgarden.ca

Proven Winners
www.provenwinners.com

Renee's Garden Seeds
www.reneesgarden.com

Urban Harvest
www.uharvest.ca

William Dam Seeds
www.damseeds.ca

IRRIGATION SYSTEMS

Les Urbainculteurs
www.urbainculteurs.org

Urban Irrigation Solutions
www.urbanirrigation.ca

LANDSCAPING COMPANIES

Fern Ridge Landscaping & Eco-Consulting
www.fernridgelandscaping.com

SOIL INFORMATION

The Compost Council of Canada
www.compost.org

Food and Agriculture Organization of the United Nations
www.fao.org

United Nations General Assembly document on World Soil Day and International Year of Soils
www.un.org/en/ga/search/view_doc.asp?symbol=A/RES/68/232&Lang=E

US Composting Council
www.compostingcouncil.org

GARDENING BLOGS AND WEBSITES

The Internet provides an endless source of ideas and inspiration. Here are some must-reads:

The Art of Doing Stuff
www.theartofdoingstuff.com

Beach Community Edible Garden
www.beachcommunitygarden.wix.com/grow

That Bloomin' Garden
www.thatbloomingarden.wordpress.com

The Bug Blog
www.jessicawalliser.com/bug-blog

Empress of Dirt
www.empressofdirt.net

#GardenChat on Twitter
www.Twitter.com/thegardenchat

Get Busy Gardening!
www.getbusygardening.com

Inside Urban Green
www.insideurbangreen.org

More Than Oregano
www.morethanoregano.com

On Blueberry Hill
www.blueberryhillcrafting.com

Orchard People
www.orchardpeople.com

Red Dirt Ramblings
www.reddirtramblings.com

The Year Round Veggie Gardener
www.yearroundveggiegardener.blogspot.ca

Tonic Toronto
www.tonictoronto.com

Three Dogs in a Garden
www.threedogsinagarden.blogspot.com

INDEX

MEET TARA NOLAN

Photo Credit: Marsha Z.

Tara Nolan is a freelance writer and editor. She loves to write about gardening (of course!) as well as her outdoorsy adventures on foot and on her mountain bike. Tara's gardening articles have appeared in the *Toronto Star*, *Canadian Living* magazine, *Reader's Digest* magazine, and other publications. She was the editor of *Canadian Gardening* magazine's website for six years, where she wrote for both the online and print publication. In 2013, Tara won the Gold award at the Canadian Online Publishing Awards for her "Seed to Supper" newsletter. The newsletter was created to inspire gardeners to grow their own food and then teach them what to do with the harvest via recipes, and cooking and preserving tips.

On the woodworking side of things, Tara was the web editor of the *Canadian Home Workshop* website, and later on, under a new owner, an associate editor and then senior editor of the print magazine for two years.

(Tara was so excited when her gardening world and woodworking world came together to make this book!)

In 2013, Tara co-founded the gardening website www.savvygardening.com with three fellow members of the Garden Writers Association: Amy Andrychowicz, Niki Jabbour, and Jessica Walliser. Together, these four green thumbs from two different countries and four different growing zones work to inspire both experienced and budding gardeners with innovative ideas, tips, and advice.

Tara also volunteers at the Royal Botanical Gardens, and she does work with the Toronto Botanical Garden and the Canadian Garden Council.

Follow Tara and her adventures in gardening online:

Raised Bed Revolution
www.raisedbedrevolution.com
Facebook.com/raisedbedrevolution

Savvy Gardening
www.savvygardening.com
www.Facebook.com/savvygardening
Twitter: @savvygardening

Tara Nolan
Twitter: @thattaranolan
Instagram: @tara_e